Integrated Chinese

中文聽說讀寫

Traditional Character Edition
Character Workbook

Tao-chung Yao, Yuehua Liu
Xiaojun Wang, Yea-fen Chen, Liangyan Ge
with Jeffrey J. Hayden

Cheng & Tsui Company

First edition
2001 printing

Cheng & Tsui Company
25 West Street
Boston, MA 02111-1213 USA

Traditional Character Edition
ISBN 0-88727-272-X

Companion textbooks, workbooks and audio tapes are also available from the publisher.

Printed in the United States of America

Integrated Chinese I, Part 2 — Character Workbook

Table of Contents

PREFACE

This *Character Workbook* is a companion volume to the *Integrated Chinese Textbook, Level 1, Part 2 (Traditional Character Version)*. *Integrated Chinese* is a series of Chinese language textbooks written by the *Integrated Chinese* committee which consists of seven members: Nyan-ping Bi, Yea-fen Chen, Liangyan Ge, Yuehua Liu, Yaohua Shi, Xiaojun Wang, and Tao-chung Yao. In addition to this *Character Workbook*, there is another workbook for students to learn the four language skills (listening, speaking, reading, and writing).

This book is designed to help the student learn Chinese characters in their correct stroke order, and then by components. We believe that the student will learn a new character more easily if s/he can identify the components in each character and know why the specific components are used. Therefore, we strongly urge teachers to teach their students the 40 basic radicals which are frequently used to compose Chinese characters. These 40 radicals are introduced in the *Character Workbook* for *Level 1, Part 1*.

When learning a new character, the student should first try to identify the known component(s). Through this process, the student need only remember a character by its components, rather than as the composition of many meaningless strokes. For example, both 女 (nǚ, female) and 馬 (mǎ, horse) are taught in the radical section. Hence, when the student sees the character 媽 (mā, mother) in Lesson 2 of Level 1, Part 1, s/he should be able to recognize its components, namely, 女 and 馬. The components in a character sometimes give clues to the meaning and pronunciation of the character. The radical 女 in the character 媽 suggests that the character might be related to females, and the other component, 馬, is a phonetic element giving a clue to its pronunciation. If a student can remember that the character for "mother" sounds like "horse," s/he will have an easier time learning how to write the character.

Explanation of Symbols

Each page of this *Character Workbook* has three to four new characters on it. Every new character is displayed in a large point size on the left side of the page, with its *pinyin* reading and English translation immediately to the right. Next to the *pinyin* reading is a number in parentheses, indicating the ranking of the character given in the <u>Xiāndài Hànyǔ Pínlǜ Cídiǎn</u> (《現代漢語頻率詞典》, *The Dictionary of Modern Chinese Word Frequency*). For example, for the character 人 (rén, person), the number "9" given in the parentheses means that this character is the ninth most frequently used character in the Chinese language.

The symbol "†" in the parentheses indicates that the character does not belong to the 1000 most frequently used characters according to the <u>Xiàndài Hànyǔ Pínlǜ Dà Cídiǎn</u>. While we try to introduce the first 1000 most frequently used characters at the first two levels of *Integrated Chinese*, we sometimes have to include some characters beyond the first thousand to make the text natural and functional.

How to Use This Workbook

In the main lessons, the simplified version of the character is given to the right of the smaller traditional character. Occasionally the character to the right will have the small symbol "Δ" after it, indicating the printing form. Students should learn how to write the written form, i.e., the character to the left of it. An asterisk (*) before an English translation means that the character is bound to another character and that the English translation represents the meaning of the compound rather than the individual character. Each practicing unit for a character contains three or four rows of small boxes. The first row has a grayed version of the character. The student should trace this. The second row is in a graph-style layout to facilitate practice at character proportion. The third row and the remaining empty boxes are for the student to practice writing the character. By this time, the student should be able to draw the character in proper spatial proportions without the use of any guides.

It is very important to draw each character in the correct stroke order. Two devices are used in this workbook to show a character's stroke order. The small numbers printed along the large characters indicate the sequence of the strokes. In general, every effort has been made to place the number at the starting point of the stroke. Because, in some instances, it is not very easy to tell which number goes with what stroke, or to tell where each stroke begins and ends, a "pen version" of each character is provided. Right below the large character, the character is drawn one step at a time to show how it is formed. Students should consult this series of strokes when practicing writing characters.

For components which have previously appeared, the pen version may simply show the entire component. For example, the pen version for the character 胖 (pàng, fat) in Lesson 20, of Level I, Part 2 only uses two boxes, one for 月, and one for 半. This means that when writing the character 胖, one first writes 月, and then one writes 半 next to 月 to form 胖. No individual strokes are given here because the student has already learned how to write 月 , and 半 separately.

There are many computer programs available (such as *Chinese Character* Tutor by Ted Yao and Mark Peterson and *Hanzi Assistant* by Panda Software) which are designed to teach stroke order. Students are encouraged to use them if they have access to the software. For additional information on computer software for learning Chinese characters, please see our home page at <http://www.lll.hawaii.edu/ICUsers/>.

The three people who have spent the most time in preparing this *Character Workbook* are Tao-Chung Yao, Jeffrey J. Hayden, and Xiaojun Wang. Yao designed the format for the first two versions (1994, 1995) and wrote the stroke numbers by hand. Wang did the calligraphy for the very first version (1994) and has also done most of the pen version stroke ordering in this current edition. Yao and Hayden collaborated on the 1996 and 1997 editions. Yao was responsible for the overall planning, and Hayden has translated Yao's ideas into the current form, including entering all of the data and numbering each stroke. We would like to thank Mr. Song Jiang for checking the stroke order and for doing the pen version stroke ordering for some of the characters in this volume.

Dialogue I

	wù (376) *service	務	務	務	務	務	務
務	務 务						
予 予 矛 矛 矛 敄 務							

	zhuō (869) table	桌	桌	桌	桌	桌	桌
桌	桌						
丿 卜 占 桌							

	cài (707) vegetable; dish	菜	菜	菜	菜	菜	
菜	菜 菜						
艹 艹 艹 茓 苎 菜							

	jiǎo (†) dumpling	餃	餃	餃	餃	餃	餃
餃	餃 饺						
食 餃							

素	sù (766) white; plain	素	素	素	素	素	素
	素						
圭	耂	素					

盤	pán (850) plate; dish	盤	盤	盤	盤	盤	盤
	盤	盘					
ノ	｀丶	力	丹	舟	舟	般	盤

豆	dòu (†) bean	豆	豆	豆	豆	豆	豆
	豆						
一	口	戸	豆	豆			

腐	fǔ (†) rotten; stale	腐	腐	腐	腐	腐	腐
	腐						
广	厂	府	府	腐	腐	腐	

肉	ròu (866) meat	肉	肉	肉	肉	肉	肉
	肉						
冂	内	肉					

碗	wǎn (996) bowl	碗	碗	碗	碗	碗	碗
	碗						
一	丆	石	矿	矽	碗	碗	

酸	suān (†) sour	酸	酸	酸	酸	酸	酸
	酸						
酉	酌	酌	酌	酸	酸	酸	

辣	là (†) hot; spicy	辣	辣	辣	辣	辣	辣
	辣						
立	辛	辛	辛	辣	辣	辣	辣

湯	tāng (†) soup	湯	湯	湯	湯	湯	湯
	湯 汤						
氵 氵 氵 湯							

放	fàng (163) to put in; to add	放	放	放	放	放	
	放						
方 放							

味	wèi (822) flavor	味	味	味	味	味	味
	味						
口 味							

精	jīng (459) essence	精	精	精	精	精	精
	精						
米 精							

渴	kě (†) thirsty		渴	渴	渴	渴	渴	渴
	渴							
氵	沪	沪	渴	渴	渴			

些	xiē (92) some		些	些	些	些	些	些
	些							
丨	卜	止	止	止	此	此	些	

夠	gòu (380) enough		夠	夠	夠	夠	夠	夠
	夠	够						
多	多	夠	夠					

餓	è (†) to be hungry		餓	餓	餓	餓	餓	餓
	餓	饿						
食	餓							

Dialogue II

傅	fù teacher (†)	傅	傅	傅	傅	傅	傅
	傅						
亻	仁	伫	佇	侕	侕	伸	傅	傅

糖	táng sugar (†)	糖	糖	糖	糖	糖	糖
	糖						
米	籿	籿	粘	粻	糖	糖		

醋	cù vinegar (†)	醋	醋	醋	醋	醋	醋
	醋						
酉	酌	酐	酣	酤	醋		

魚	yú fish (537)	魚	魚	魚	魚	魚	魚
	魚	鱼					
勹	龟	魚					

甜	tián (†)	甜	甜	甜	甜	甜	甜
	sweet						
	甜						
丶	二	千	舌	舌	甜	甜	甜	甜

極	jí (389)	極	極	極	極	極	極
	extreme						
	極	极					
木	村	朽	桮	極	極		

燒	shāo (684)	燒	燒	燒	燒	燒	燒
	to burn, cook						
	燒	烧					
火	灶	烨	烨	烨	烨	燒	

牛	niú (779)	牛	牛	牛	牛	牛	牛
	cow; ox						
	牛						
丿	丶	二	牛				

賣	mài (591) to sell	賣	賣	賣	賣	賣	賣	賣
	賣 卖							
士 吉 賣								

完	wán (251) to finish	完	完	完	完	完	完	完
	完							
宀 宀 㝉 宇 完								

拌	bàn (†) mix	拌	拌	拌	拌	拌	拌	拌
	拌							
扌 拌								

瓜	guā (†) melon	瓜	瓜	瓜	瓜	瓜	瓜	瓜
	瓜							
一 厂 爪 瓜 瓜								

米	mǐ rice (430)	米	米	米	米	米	米
	米						
丶	丷	丷	半	半	米		

Dialogue I

		jiè (†) to borrow	借	借	借	借	借	借
借		借						
	亻	件	借					

		dài (261) belt; tape	帶	帶	帶	帶	帶	帶
帶		帶	帶					
	一	十	廿	卅	卅	卅	卅	帶

		zhí (†) duty; job	職	職	職	職	職	職
職 *see page 103*		職	职					
	耳	耵	睹	職				

		bǎ (57) Preposition	把	把	把	把	把	把
把		把						
	扌	把						

證	zhèng (584) evidence; certificate	證	證	證	證	證
	證	证				
言	訂	詼	證			

留	liú (616) leave (behind); remain; stay	留	留	留	留	
	留					
㇀	㇀	幺	幼	留		

言	yán (655) word	言	言	言	言	言	言
	言						
言							

實	shí (109) reality	實	實	實	實	實	實
	實	实					
宀	宀	宀	宲	宲	實		

驗 *see page 103*	yàn (443) to examine; to check		驗	驗	驗	驗	驗
	驗	验					
馬	馭	馬	馬	馬	馬	驗	

樓	lóu (†) floor; storey		樓	樓	樓	樓	樓	樓
	樓	楼					
木	木	杆	杆	栯	椙	楎	樓

忘	wàng (810) to forget		忘	忘	忘	忘	忘	忘
	忘						
丶	亠	亡	忘				

其	qí (253) he; she; it; they		其	其	其	其	其
	其					
一	十	艹	廿	甘	且	其	其

卡	kǎ (†) to block; to check	卡	卡	卡	卡	卡
	卡					
丿	卜	上	卡	卡			

關	guān (203) to close	關	關	關	關	關	關
	關	关					
門	閂	鬥	鬥	鬦	鬪	關	關

門	mén (199) door; gate	門	門	門	門	門	門
	門	门					
丨	冂	冂	門	門	門	門	門

剩	shèng (†) to remain; to be left over	剩	剩	剩	剩	
	剩					
一	二	千	千	乒	乖	乖	乖	乘
乘	剩							

頭	tóu (75) head	頭	頭	頭	頭	頭	頭
	頭 头						
豆 頭							

及	jí (465) reach	及	及	及	及	及	及
	及						
ノ 了 乃 及							

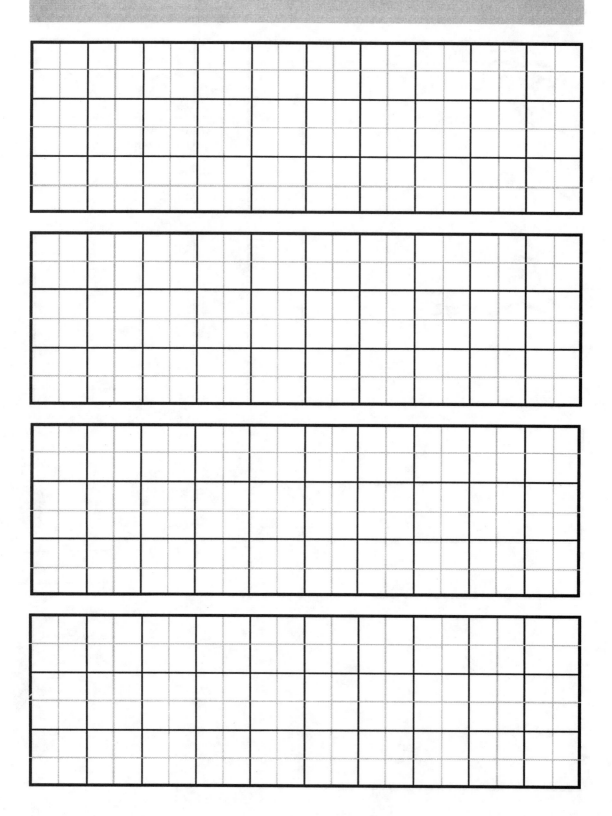

Dialogue II

本	běn (138) M (for books)	本	本	本	本	本	本
	本						
一	十	才	木	本			

如	rú (145) like; as if	如	如	如	如	如	如
	如						
く	夕	女	如				

果	guǒ (223) fruit; result	果	果	果	果	果	果
	果						
丨	冂	曰	日	旦	甲	畢	果

罰	fá (†) to fine; to punish	罰	罰	罰	罰	罰	
	罰	罚					
丶	冂	罒	罒	罒	詈	罰	

繪	xù (637) to continue; to extend	績	績	績	績	績
see page 103	繪	续				
幺	糸	繪	繪	繪		

必	bì (337) must	必	必	必	必	必	必
	必					
✓	八	心	必	必		

須	xū (476) must	須	須	須	須	須	須
	須	须				
ノ	ク	彡	彡	彡	須	

典	diǎn (†) standard work	典	典	典	典	典
	典					
丨	冂	曰	由	曲	曲	典	典

Dialogue I

	yùn (301) to carry; to transport	運	運	運	運	運
運	運 运					
冖 軍 運						

	dòng (58) to move; to stir	動	動	動	動	動
動	動 动					
丿 二 旨 車 車 重 動						

	páng (645) side	旁	旁	旁	旁	旁	旁
旁	旁						
丶 亠 六 六 六 产 旁							

	yuǎn (341) far; distant; remote	遠	遠	遠	遠	遠
遠	遠 远					
土 吉 吉 责 袁 袁 遠						

住	zhù (201) to live (at)	住	住	住	住	住	住
	住						
亻	亻	住					

離 *see page 103*	lí (426) from; away	離	離	離	離	離	離
	離	离					
、	亠	亠	文	辶	卤	卢	㡿	离	离
離							

活	huó (88) to live	活	活	活	活	活	活
	活						
氵	氵	汙	汙	活			

心	xīn (82) heart	心	心	心	心	心	心
	心						
丶	八	心	心				

店	diàn (817) store; shop		店	店	店	店	店	店
	店							
广	广	广	店					

田	tián (727) (a surname); field		田	田	田	田	田
	田						
丨	冂	冃	田	田			

金	jīn (514) (a surname); gold; metal		金	金	金	金
	金					
丿	人	人	今	全	全	金	金

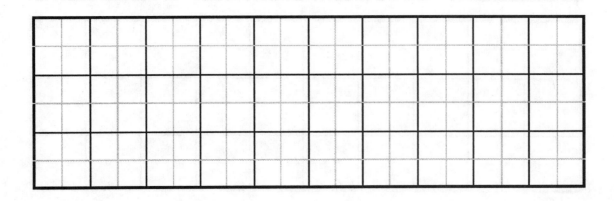

Dialogue II

城	chéng (528) city; town	城	城	城	城	城	城
	城						
土	圵	圹	坊	城	城	城	

閉	bì (†) to close	閉	閉	閉	閉	閉	閉
	閉	闭					
門	閂	閅	閉				

著	zhe (18) P	著	著	著	著	著	著
	著	着					
艹	艹	芊	芏	茅	著		

眼	yǎn (148) eye	眼	眼	眼	眼	眼	眼
	眼						
目	目	目	目	眼	眼	眼	

睛	jīng (493) eyeball	睛	睛	睛	睛	睛	睛
	睛						
目　睛							

從	cóng (89) from	從	從	從	從	從	從
	從　从						
ノ　ク　彳　彳　從　從　從　從　從							

直	zhí (274) straight	直	直	直	直	直	直
	直　直						
一　十　广　方　方　直　直　直							

往	wàng / wǎng (†) towards	往	往	往	往	往	
	往						
彳　往							

南	nán (456) south	南		南	南	南	南	南	南
	南								
一	十	冂	内	内	南	南	南		

拐	guǎi (†) to turn	拐		拐	拐	拐	拐	拐	拐
	拐								
才	扣	拐							

哎	āi (885) Excl.	哎	哎	哎	哎	哎	哎	哎	哎
	哎	哎							
口	口艹	哎	哎						

燈	dēng (571) light; lamp	燈		燈	燈	燈	燈	燈	燈
	燈	灯							
火	火灬	燈							

	yòu (642) right	右	右	右	右	右	右
	右						
一	ナ	右					

	dān (501) one; single; odd	單	單	單	單	單	
	單	单					
ㅁ	吅	甼	眔	單			

	zuǒ (575) left	左	左	左	左	左	左
	左						
一	ナ	左					

	miàn (68) face; side	面	面	面	面	面	面
	面						
一	丆	厂	丏	而	而	面	面

京	jīng (t) capital		京	京	京	京	京	京
	京							
、	一	亠	京					

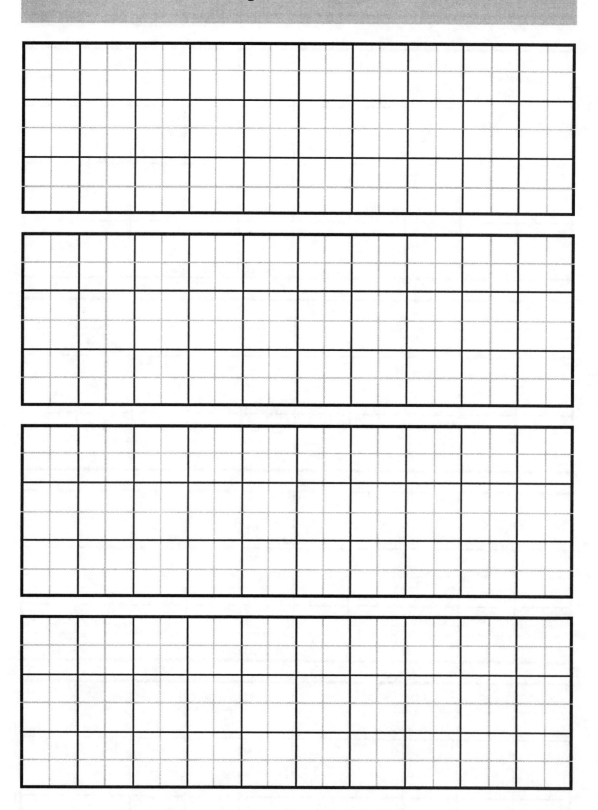

Dialogue I

	biǎo (221) outside; form	表	表	表	表	表	表
表	表						
一	二	圭	主	丰	表	表	表

	bān (703) class	班	班	班	班	班	班
班	班						
王	玎	玐	班				

	zhī (†) juice	汁	汁	汁	汁	汁	汁
汁	汁						
氵	汁	汁					

	jiē (279) to meet; to receive	接	接	接	接	接	
接	接						
扌	扌	扩	拧	护	拉	接	

林	lín (721) (a surname); forest	林	林	林	林	林
	林					
一	十	才	木	林		

Dialogue II

禮	lǐ (†) ceremony	禮	禮	禮	禮	禮	禮
	禮 礼						
`	⁓	⼂	⽰	礻	初	初	袖 袖 袖
袖 禮 禮 禮 禮							

物	wù (132) thing	物	物	物	物	物	物
	物						
ノ	⼂	牛	牛	牛	牜	物	物

聰 see page 103	cōng (†) acute hearing	聰	聰	聰	聰	聰	聰
	聰 聪						
耳	耳	耴	耴	耴	聏	聦	聦 聰

暑	shǔ (†) heat; hot weather		暑	暑	暑	暑	暑
	暑						
曰	旦	早	星	暑	暑		

長	zhǎng / cháng (100) to grow; to look / long	長	長	長	長	長
	長 长					
一	丨	⼲	乍	耳	丟	長 長

愛	ài (312) to love	愛	愛	愛	愛	愛	愛
	愛 爱						
一	㇒	㇒	爫	爫	哑	恶	恶 爱 愛

屬 see page 103	shǔ (†) to belong to	屬	屬	屬	屬	屬	屬
	屬 属						
㇕	ㄱ	尸	尸	尽	尿	屌	屌 属 屬
屬 屬 屬							

狗	gǒu (1000) dog	狗	狗	狗	狗	狗	狗
	狗						
ノ	㇇	犭	犭	狗	狗		

鼻	bí (†) nose	鼻	鼻	鼻	鼻	鼻	鼻
	鼻						
丿	自	畠	畠	鼻	鼻		

嘴	zuǐ (520) mouth	嘴	嘴	嘴	嘴	嘴	嘴
	嘴						
口	口丨	口卜	口止	口此	口此	口此	嘴 嘴 嘴

將	jiāng (295) to be going to	將	將	將	將	將	將
	將 將						
㇄	丬	丬	爿	爿	爿	爿	爿 將

定	dìng (121) to decide; to fix; to set	定	定	定	定	定	
	定						
丶	宀	宀	宁	宁	宇	定	

臉	liǎn (365) face	臉	臉	臉	臉	臉	臉
	臉 脸						
月	肶	胎	胎	脸	脸	臉	臉

腿	tuǐ (852) leg	腿	腿	腿	腿	腿	腿
	腿						
月	月ㄱ	月ㄱ	月ㄢ	肥	肥	服	服	腿	腿

指	zhǐ (272) finger	指	指	指	指	指	指
	指						
扌	扌	扩	指	指			

應	yīng (215) should; ought to	應	應	應	應	應
see page 104	應 应					
广	厂	庐	庐	庐	庐	庐	雁	雁	應

該	gāi (354) should; ought to	該	該	該	該	該
	該 该					
言	言	訁	訡	該	該	

彈	tán (698) to play	彈	彈	彈	彈	彈	彈
	彈 弹						
フ	フ	弓	弻	弻	弻	彊	彈

鋼	gāng (573) steel	鋼	鋼	鋼	鋼	鋼	鋼
	鋼 钢						
金	釒	釘	釘	鋼	鋼	鋼	鋼

琴	qín (†) stringed instrument	琴	琴	琴	琴	琴
	琴					
王	珏	珡	琴	琴		

倫	lún (t) relationship	倫	倫	倫	倫	倫	倫
	倫　伦						
亻	伫	伶	价	伶	伶	倫	倫

姆	mǔ (t) *nurse; *maid	姆	姆	姆	姆	姆	
	姆						
女	奻	奵	奵	姆	姆		

Dialogue I

病	bìng (424) illness	病	病	病	病	病	病
	病						
广	广	疒	疒	疒	病	病	病

肚	dù (†) stomach; belly	肚	肚	肚	肚	肚	
	肚						
月	肚						

疼	téng (†) to be painful	疼	疼	疼	疼	疼	疼
	疼						
疒	疒	疒	疚	疼	疼		

死	sǐ (356) to die	死	死	死	死	死	死
	死						
一	歹	死					

廁	cè (†) lavatory; toilet; W.C.	廁	廁	廁	廁	廁
	廁	厕				
广	庍	廁				

躺	tǎng (†) to lie down	躺	躺	躺	躺	躺	躺
	躺						
ノ	亻	亻	身	身	身	躯	躯	躬	躺

檢	jiǎn (768) to inspect; to examine	檢	檢	檢	檢
	檢	检			
木	檢				

查	chá (†) to inspect; to examine	查	查	查	查
	查				
木	杳	查			

	huài (544) bad	壞	壞	壞	壞	壞	壞
壞 see page 104	壞 坏						
土 扩	坪 坪	坪	坪	坪	壞	壞	壞
壞 壞							

	zhēn (771) needle	針	針	針	針	針	針
針	針 针						
金 金 針							

	zhǒng (86) kind; type	種	種	種	種	種	種
種	種 种						
禾 種							

	yào (629) medicine	藥	藥	藥	藥	藥	藥
藥	藥 药						
艹 艹 苩 茹 蓹 藥							

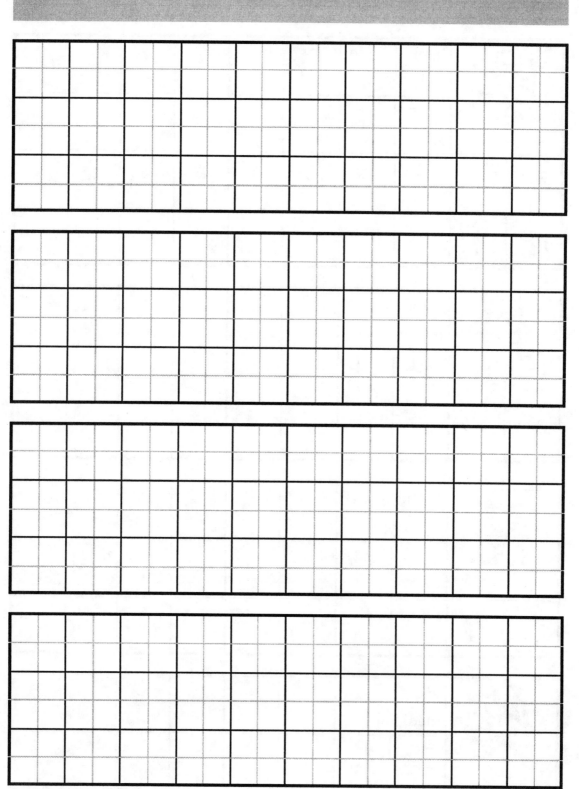

Dialogue II

	lèi (964) tear	涙	涙	涙	涙	涙	涙
涙	涙 泪						
氵 氵 沪 涙 涙							

	liú (278) to flow; to shed	流	流	流	流	流	
流	流						
氵 汀 汸 泸 済 流							

	shēn (155) body	身	身	身	身	身	身
身	身						
丿 亻 门 勺 月 身 身							

	tǐ (191) body	體	體	體	體	體	體
體 see page 104	體 体						
丶 冂 冂 回 皿 骨 體 體							

癢 see page 104	yǎng (†) to itch	癢	癢	癢	癢	癢	癢
	癢　痒						
广　痒　疒　痒　癢							

敏	mǐn (†) quick; nimble; agile	敏	敏	敏	敏	敏	
	敏						
每　敏							

趕	gǎn (504) hurry; rush	趕	趕	趕	趕	趕	趕
	趕　赶						
土　走　趕　趕　趕　趕							

越	yuè (382) exceed; overlap	越	越	越	越	越	
	越						
土　走　走　起　越　越							

重	zhòng (153) serious; heavy	重	重	重	重	重
	重					
丿	二	言	盲	重	重	

(Please note that stroke 1 goes down from right to left.)

健	jiàn (†) healthy; strong	健	健	健	健	健
	健					
亻	亻丶	仁	仨	侓	侓	律	律	健

康	kāng (†) well-being; health	康	康	康	康	康
	康					
广	广	庐	庐	庐	庚	庚	康	康

保	bǎo (400) to protect; to defend	保	保	保	保	保
	保					
亻	伫	保				

險	xiǎn (†) danger; risk	險	險	險	險	險	險
	險	险					
了	阝	險					

猜	cāi (†) to guess	猜	猜	猜	猜	猜	猜
	猜						
犭	猜						

馬	mǎ (359) (a surname); horse	馬	馬	馬	馬	馬	
	馬	马					
馬							

Dialogue I

參	cān (564) to participate	參	參	參	參	參	參
	參 參						
ㄥ	ㄥ	ㄥ	叕	參			

加	jiā (189) to add	加	加	加	加	加	加
	加						
力	加						

印	yìn (812) seal; stamp	印	印	印	印	印	印
	印						
一	乚	ㅌ	臼	印			

象	xiàng (107) appearance	象	象	象	象	象	象
	象						
ㄅ	由	象					

演	yǎn (778) to show; to perform	演	演	演	演	演
	演					
シ	氵	沪	洁	涫	演	演

費	fèi (756) spend; take (effort)	費	費	費	費	費
	費	费				
一	二	弓	弗	弗	費	

力	lì (119) power; strength	力	力	力	力	力
	力					
力						

倆	liǎ (†) M; two (people)	倆	倆	倆	倆	倆
	倆	倆				
亻	倆					

Dialogue II

	mǎ (†) number	碼	碼	碼	碼	碼	碼
碼	碼 码						
石	碼						

	jù (†) play; opera	劇	劇	劇	劇	劇	劇
劇	劇 剧						
丨	广	上	广	卢	虍	豦	劇

	qìng (†) celebrate	慶	慶	慶	慶	慶	慶
慶 see page 104	慶 庆						
广	广	庐	庐	庐	庶	應	廖 慶

	sǎo (†) to sweep	掃	掃	掃	掃	掃	掃
掃	掃 扫						
扌	扣	扫	扫	掃	掃		

房	fáng (440) house; room	房	房	房	房	房	房
	房						
户 房							

整	zhěng (395) neat; tidy	整	整	整	整	整	整
	整						
束 敕 整							

理	lǐ (133) to tidy up; to put in order			理	理	理	理
	理						
王 理							

旅	lǚ (†) to travel	旅	旅	旅	旅	旅	旅
	旅						
方 方 斿 斿 旅 旅							

	niǔ (†)	紐	紐	紐	紐	紐	紐
	button						
紐	紐 纽						
糸	糿	紐	紐	紐			

	xì (268)	係	係	係	係	係	係
	connection						
係	係 系						
亻	亻	伝	係				

Narrative

吵	chǎo noisy	(†)	吵	吵	吵	吵	吵	吵
	吵							
口	口小	吵						

連	lián even	(328)	連	連	連	連	連	連
	連	连						
車	連							

準	zhǔn accurate	(404)	準	準	準	準	準	準
	準	准						
冫	淮	淮	準					

備	bèi to prepare	(432)	備	備	備	備	備	備
	備	备						
亻	仁	仕	伊	俌	俌	備		

搬	bān (†) to move	搬	搬	搬	搬	搬	搬
	搬						
扌	捌	搬					

紙	zhǐ (623) paper	紙	紙	紙	紙	紙	紙
	紙	纸					
幺	幺	糹	紅	紙			

廣	guǎng (524) broad; vast	廣	廣	廣	廣	廣	廣
	廣	广					
广	庀	庐	層	廣			

(Note: Please note that the character here and the one in the textbook are slightly different due to restrictions with the computer.)

附	fù (†) get close to; be near to	附	附	附	附
	附				
阝	阝	附			

寓	yù (†) to reside; to live (at)	寓	寓	寓	寓	寓
	寓					
宀	宀	宀	宭	寓	寓	寓

里	lǐ (26) li (a Chn unit of length)	里	里	里	里	
	里					
日	甲	甲	里			

套	tào (524) set / suite	套	套	套	套	套	套
	套						
大	太	夵	夵	套	套	套	套

臥	wò (†) to lie (down)	臥	臥	臥	臥	臥	臥
	臥 卧						
臣	臥						

廚 (1-15)	chú (†) kitchen	廚	廚	廚	廚	廚	廚
see page 104	廚 厨						
广 庄 唐 唐 唐 唐 廚							

傢 (1-12)	jiā (†) *furniture	傢	傢	傢	傢	傢	傢
	傢 家						
亻 伫 傢							

俱 (1-10)	jù (450) all; complete	俱	俱	俱	俱	俱	俱
	俱 具						
亻 们 们 伯 俱 俱 俱 俱 俱							

Dialogue

沙	shā (649) sand	沙	沙	沙	沙	沙	沙	沙
	沙							
⺡	沙	沙						

椅	yǐ (†) chair	椅	椅	椅	椅	椅	椅	椅
	椅							
木	杧	椅						

架	jià (806) frame; shelf	架	架	架	架	架	架	
	架							
力	加	架						

安	ān (488) peaceful; quiet	安	安	安	安	安	
	安						
宀	安						

靜	jìng (597) quiet; calm	静	静	静	静	静	静
	靜 静						
青	青	青	青	静	静	静	

非	fēi (497) not; no	非	非	非	非	非	非
	非						
ノ	ナ	扌	丰	扌ト	非	非	非

元	yuán (776) *yuan* (a Chn unit of currency)	元	元	元	元		
	元						
一	二	テ	元				

押	yā (†) to pawn; give as security	押	押	押	押		
	押						
扌	扣	押					

當	dāng (130) to serve as; to be		當	當	當	當	當
	當	当					
㇕	㇖	⺌	⺌	㞢	當		

許	xǔ (256) to allow; to be allowed		許	許	許	許	
	許	许					
言	許						

養	yǎng (624) to raise		養	養	養	養	養	養
	養	养						
丷	羊	美	養					

Dialogue I

郵	yóu (†) mail; post	郵	郵	郵	郵	郵	郵
	郵 邮						
一	二	千	手	垂	垂	垂	郵

局	jú (594) office; bureau	局	局	局	局	局	局
	局						
尸	尸	局					

寄	jì (†) to mail; to send by mail	寄	寄	寄	寄
	寄				
宀	宊	寄			

營	yíng (†) to operate; to run	營	營	營	營	營
	營 营					
火	炏	炏	營	營	營	

貼	tiē (t) to paste on; to stick on	貼	貼	貼	貼
	貼	貼						
貝	貼							

掛	guà (877) to hang	掛	掛	掛	掛	掛	掛
	掛	挂									
扌	扗	挂	掛								

另	lìng (660) other	另	另	另	另	另	另
	另							
口	另							

Dialogue II

首	shǒu (563) head	首	首	首	首	首	首
	首						
丶	丷	丷	首				

飾	shì (†) decorations	飾	飾	飾	飾	飾	飾
	飾	饰					
食	飠	飾					

鮮	xiān (946) fresh	鮮	鮮	鮮	鮮	鮮	鮮
	鮮	鲜					
魚	魚	魚	魚	鮮	鮮	鮮	

束	shù (967) M; a bunch of (flowers, etc.)	束	束	束	束
	束				
一	戸	市	束	束	

	dìng *(t)* to order; to subscribe to	訂	訂	訂	訂
訂	訂	订				
言	言	訂				

	shōu (428) to receive	收	收	收	收	收	收
收	收						
㇄	丩	收					

	cún (630) to store; to keep	存	存	存	存	存
存	存					
一	ナ	オ	存			

	zhī (498) to pay out	支	支	支	支	支	支
支	支						
十	圡	支					

它	tā (113) it	它	它	它	它	它	它
	它						
宀	宀	它					

民	mín (67) people	民	民	民	民	民	民
	民						
コ	コ	尸	尸	民			

幣	bì (†) currency	幣	幣	幣	幣	幣	幣
	幣	帀					
㇑	㇚	㇛	丷	肖	浒	尚	尚
敝	幣						

(Note: Strokes 1 and 6 are two separate strokes.)

銀	yín (856) silver	銀	銀	銀	銀	銀	銀
	銀	银					
金	金	釒	釖	釦	銀	銀	

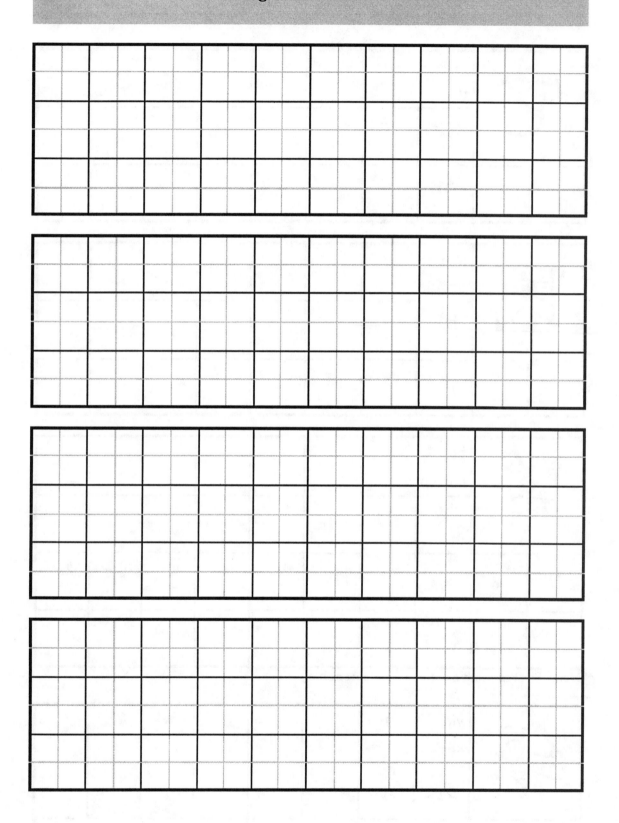

Dialogue I

胖	pàng (†) fat 胖	胖	胖	胖	胖	胖	胖
月　胖							

簡	jiǎn (656) simple 簡　简	簡	簡	簡	簡	簡	簡
竹　简　簡							

跑	pǎo (369) to run 跑	跑	跑	跑	跑	跑	跑
昆　罗　彭　趵　跑　跑							

受	shòu (330) to bear; to receive 受	受	受	受	受	受	
一　爫　爫　爫　爫　受							

網	wǎng　　(†) net	網	網	網	網	網	網
	網　网						
糸	糹	糿	納	網	網	網	網	網

拍	pāi　　(972) racket; to slap	拍	拍	拍	拍	拍	拍
	拍						
扌	拍						

籃	lán　　(†) basket	籃	籃	籃	籃	籃	籃
see page 105	籃　篮						
⺮	⺮	竻	笁	笁	笁	筲	篦	籃

游	yóu　　(676) to swim	游	游	游	游	游
	游					
氵	汸	汸	游			

泳	yǒng (†) to swim	泳	泳	泳	泳	泳	泳
	泳						
氵	氵	汀	汋	汯	泳				

危	wēi (801) danger; peril	危	危	危	危	危	危
	危						
ㄅ	ㄊ	产	危	危					

淹	yān (†) to flood; to submerge	淹	淹	淹	淹	淹
	淹					
氵	氿	淊	淹					

願	yuàn (577) be willing	願	願	願	願	願	願
	願	愿					
厂	盾	原	願					

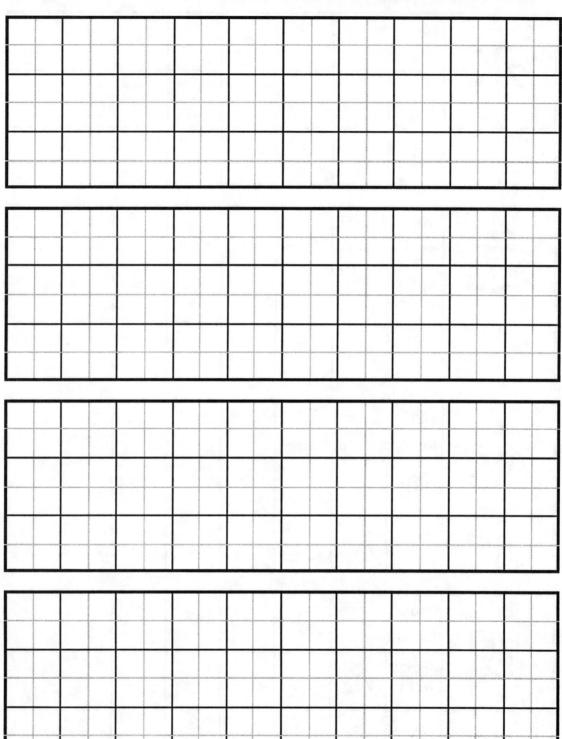

Dialogue II

調	tiáo (479) to change; to adjust; to mix		調	調	調	調
	調	调				
言	訂	調	調			

足	zú (758) foot		足	足	足	足	足	足
	足							
口	尸	尸	尺	足				

賽	sài (†) game; match; competition		賽	賽	賽	賽
	賽	賽				
宀	宀	宀	宑	审	寉	宲	寒	賽

圓	yuán (941) round		圓	圓	圓	圓	圓	圓
	圓	圆						
丨	冂	冋	圓	圓				

際	jì (480) border; edge	際	際	際	際	際	際
	際　际						
阝	阝′	阝	阝	阝	阝′	阝⁅	際	際	

式	shì (540) style; type	式	式	式	式	式	式
	式						
一	工	式	式				

腳	jiǎo (484) foot	腳	腳	腳	腳	腳	腳
	腳　脚						
月	月	月′	肤	胳	胳	腳′	腳	

踢	tī (†) to kick	踢	踢	踢	踢	踢	踢
	踢						
足	距	踢					

手	shǒu (115) hand	手	手	手	手	手	手
	手						
一	二	三	手				

抱	bào (838) to hold; to hug	抱	抱	抱	抱	抱	
	抱						
扌	抱						

壓	yā (511) to crush; to press down	壓	壓	壓	壓		
see page 105	壓 压						
厂	厈	厃	厭	厭	壓		

被	bèi (242) Preposition	被	被	被	被	被	被
	被						
礻	衤	初	衳	被			

擔	dān (696) to carry (on a shoulder)	擔	擔	擔	擔
	擔	担				
扌	扩	护	护	换	擔		

棒	bàng (忄) strong; good	棒	棒	棒	棒	棒	棒
	棒						
木	朾	栌	杵	栌	桡	榛	棒	棒

特	tè (326) special; particular	特	特	特	特	特
	特					
ノ	ヒ	牛	牛	牜	特		

傷	shāng (667) to injure; to hurt	傷	傷	傷	傷	傷
	傷	伤				
亻	仃	佰	倬	傷		

	shū (†) to lose (a game, etc.)		輸	輸	輸	輸	輸
輸	輸	輸					
	車	軒	軡	輪	輸		

	yíng (†) to win (a game, etc.)		贏	贏	贏	贏	贏
贏 *see page 105*	贏	贏					
	亡	言	声	贏	贏	贏	贏

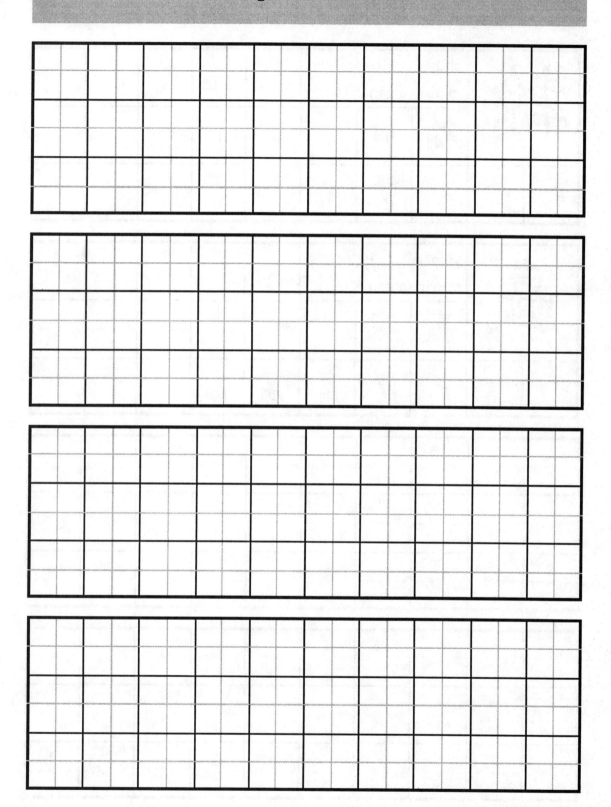

Dialogue I

計	jì (322) to count; to compute	計	計	計	計	計
	計 计					
言 計						

劃	huà (599) to plan; to delimit	劃	劃	劃	劃	劃
	劃 划					
聿 書 畫 劃						

各	gè (204) each; every	各	各	各	各	各	各
	各						
丿 ク 夂 各							

護	hù (625) to protect	護	護	護	護	護	護
	護 护						
言 訁 謢 護							

簽	qiān (†) to sign	簽	簽	簽	簽	簽	簽
	簽 簽						
⺮ 簽							

航	háng (†) boat; ship; to navigate	航	航	航	航
	航				
舟 舟 舫 航					

司	sī (816) to manage; to attend to	司	司	司	司
	司				
𠃌 㕌 司					

減	jiǎn (835) to reduce; to decrease	減	減	減	減	減
	減 減					
氵 氵 氵 沪 沪 減 減 減						

價	jià (647) price; value	價	價	價	價	價	價
	價 价						
亻 俨 價							

社	shè (137) community; society	社	社	社	社	社	
	社						
礻 社							

程	chéng (416) rule; order; journey	程	程	程	程	程	
	程						
禾 和 程							

折	zhé (†) to break; to discount	折	折	折	折	折	
	折						
扌 折							

頓	dùn (†) M (for meals)	頓	頓	頓	頓	頓
	頓	頓				
一	匸	屽	屯	頓		

華	huá (†) magnificent; China	華	華	華	華	華
	華	华				
十	艹	芣	芣	芀	莕	莊	莛	華

(Note: Strokes 7 and 9 are separate strokes.)

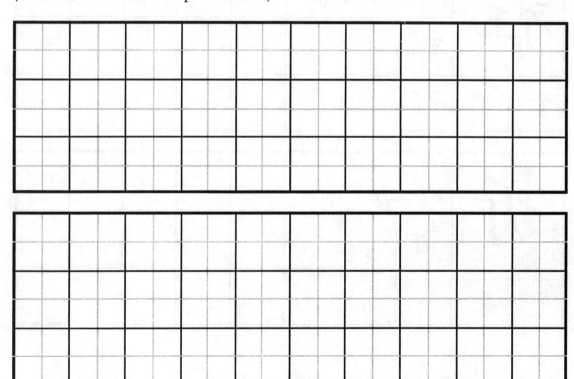

Dialogue II

初	chū (680) first; beginning	初	初	初	初	初
	初					
衤	初					

千	qiān (407) thousand	千	千	千	千	千	千
	千						
丿	千						

轉	zhuǎn (343) to turn	轉	轉	轉	轉	轉	轉
	轉	转					
車	輔	轉	轉	轉			

內	nèi (246) inside	內	內	內	內	內	內
	內						
丨	冂	內	內				

漲 zhǎng	(†) to rise	漲	漲	漲	漲	漲	漲
	漲 涨						
氵 冴 漲							

盛 shèng	(†) flourishing; abundant	盛	盛	盛	盛		
	盛						
成 盛							

韓 hán	(†) (a surname); Korea	韓	韓	韓	韓	韓	
see page 105	韓 韩						
十	吉	堇	堇?	堇?	韋	韔	韔	韔	韓

芝 zhī	(†) *sesame (seed)	芝	芝	芝	芝	芝	
	芝 芝						
艹	艹	芝	芝				

洛	luò (†) (name of a river)	洛	洛	洛	洛	洛
	洛					
氵	洛					

杉	shān (†) China fir	杉	杉	杉	杉	杉	杉
	杉						
木	杉						

磯	jī (†) a rock over water	磯	磯	磯	磯	磯
	磯 矶					
石	磯					

香	xiāng (959) fragrant	香	香	香	香	香	香
	香						
一	二	千	禾	禾	香		

港	gǎng (†) port; harbor	港	港	港	港	港	港
	港						
氵	艹	沣	洪	浒	浐	港			

Integrated Chinese

Lesson 22

Dialogue I

父	fù (614) father	父	父	父	父	父	父
	父						
′ ′′ ′′′ 父							

母	mǔ (472) mother	母	母	母	母	母	母
	母						
ㄥ 口 母 母 母							

婆	pó (†) old woman	婆	婆	婆	婆	婆	婆
	婆						
シ ジ ジ 沙 波 婆							

阿	ā (†) Prefix	阿	阿	阿	阿	阿	阿
	阿						
ㄅ 阿							

姨	yí (†) aunt	姨	姨	姨	姨	姨	姨
	姨						
女	女	奵	姨				

親	qīn (241) related by blood	親	親	親	親	親	
	親	亲					
亲	親						

戚	qī (†) relative	戚	戚	戚	戚	戚	戚
	戚						
一	厂	厃	庈	底	戚	戚	

伯	bó (†) uncle	伯	伯	伯	伯	伯	伯
	伯						
亻	伯						

市	shì (461) city; market	市	市	市	市	市	市
	市						
、	一	市					

鄉	xiāng (634) countryside	鄉	鄉	鄉	鄉	鄉	鄉
	鄉	乡					
㇀	㇀	乡	乡	纟	纟	绊	绊	绑	鄉

啦	lā (†) P	啦	啦	啦	啦	啦	啦
	啦						
口	呌	啦					

鎮	zhèn (990) town	鎮	鎮	鎮	鎮	鎮	鎮
	鎮	鎮	镇				
金	釒	釒	釖	鉬	鉬	鉬	鎮	鎮	鎮

座	zuò (694) M (for bridges, mountains)	座	座	座	座		
	座						
广	庁	庅	庍	座	座		

山	shān (193) mountain	山	山	山	山	山	山
	山						
丨	凵	山					

河	hé (360) river	河	河	河	河	河	河
	河						
氵	河						

樹	shù (401) tree	樹	樹	樹	樹	樹	樹
	樹	树					
木	术	桔	楂	樹			

滿	mǎn (349) full	滿	滿	滿	滿	滿	滿
	滿	滿					
シ	沖	沖	沛	滿	滿	滿	滿	滿

風	fēng (262) wind	風	風	風	風	風	風
	風	风					
丿	几	凡	凧	風	風	風		

景	jǐng (811) scenery; scene	景	景	景	景	景
	景					
日	景					

季	jì (987) season	季	季	季	季	季	季
	季						
禾	季						

滑	huá (†) to slide	滑	滑	滑	滑	滑	滑
	滑						
氵	汀	汈	汈	滑	滑				

雪	xuě (627) snow	雪	雪	雪	雪	雪	雪
	雪						
雨	雪	雪	雪						

迎	yíng (958) to welcome	迎	迎	迎	迎	迎	迎
	迎						
丶	㇀	印	印	迎					

州	zhōu (†) state	州	州	州	州	州	州
	州						
丶	丿	氿	州	州	州				

舊 jiù old (622) see page 105	舊	旧	舊	舊	舊	舊	舊	舊

| 𦫫 | 萑 | 萑 | 萑 | 萑 | 舊 | 舊 | 舊 | | |

Dialogue II

較	jiào (448) to compare	較	較	較	較	較	較
	較 较						
車 較							

政	zhèng (196) politics	政	政	政	政	政	政
	政						
正 政							

濟	jì (368) to help; to benefit	濟	濟	濟	濟	濟	
	濟 济						
氵 氵 氵 氵 氵 济 济 济 济 济							
済 済 濟							

部	bù (117) part; section	部	部	部	部	部	部
	部						
立 音 部							

颳 (guā)	guā (†) to blow	颳	颳	颳	颳	颳	颳
	颳 刮						
風 颳							

導 (dǎo)	dǎo (265) to lead; to guide	導	導	導	導	導	
	導 导						
see page 105 丶 丷 丷 首 道 導							

遊 (yóu)	yóu (†) to travel; to tour	遊	遊	遊	遊	遊	
	遊 游						
方 方 游 遊							

Dialogue I

探	tàn (†) to visit	探	探	探	探	探	探
	探						
扌	扩	护	护	抨	探		

拾	shí (†) to pick up	拾	拾	拾	拾	拾	拾
	拾						
扌	扑	拎	拾				

提	tí (231) to carry; to raise	提	提	提	提	提
	提					
扌	押	提				

醒	xǐng (†) to wake up	醒	醒	醒	醒	醒	醒
	醒						
酉	酉卩	醒					

差	chà (722) wanting; short of	差	差	差	差	差
	差					
半 半 差						

停	tíng (598) to park; to stop	停	停	停	停	停
	停					
亻 亻 信 停 停 停						

托	tuō (†) to ask; to entrust	托	托	托	托	托
	托					
扌 扌 扦 托						

皮	pí (533) skin; leather	皮	皮	皮	皮	皮	皮
	皮						
一 厂 广 皮							

箱	xiāng (⺮) box; case; trunk	箱	箱	箱	箱	箱
	箱					
⺮	笁	箱				

隨	suí (518) to follow	隨	隨	隨	隨	隨	隨
	隨	随					
阝	阝一	阼	陸	隋	隨		

拿	ná (327) to take	拿	拿	拿	拿	拿	拿
	拿						
人	人	合	拿				

稱	chēng (728) to weigh	稱	稱	稱	稱	稱	稱
	稱	称					
禾	禾	禾	秒	秒	秤	稻	稀	稱	稱

	chāo　　(†) to exceed; to surpass		超	超	超	超	超
超	超						
土	走	起	超				

	dēng　　(†) to board		登	登	登	登	登	登
登	登							
癶	登							

	jí　　(500) urgent; pressing		急	急	急	急	急
急	急						
⺈	刍	急					

	kū　　(738) to cry		哭	哭	哭	哭	哭	哭
哭	哭							
口	吅	哭	哭					

途	tú (辶) road; way	途	途	途	途	途	途
	途						
人	余	途					

順	shùn (830) in the same direction	順	順	順	順	順
	順	順				
丿	川	川	順			

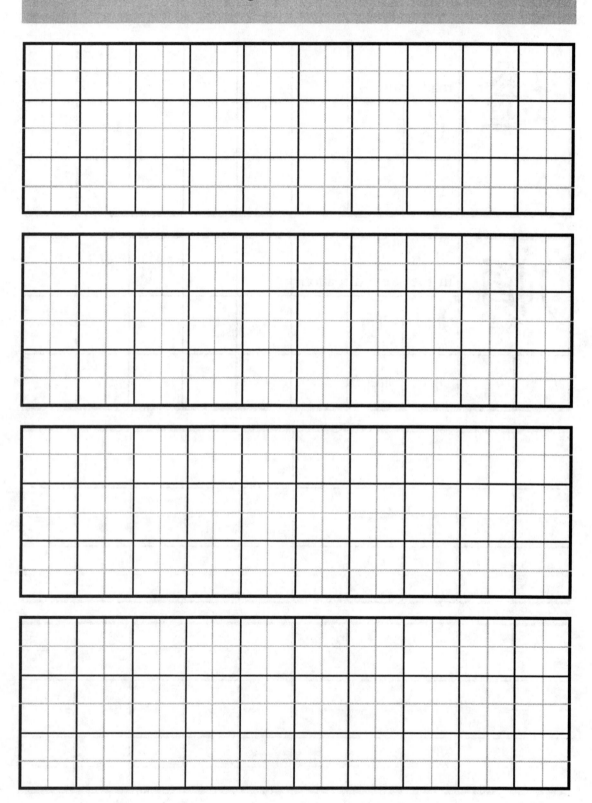

Dialogue II

辛	xīn (†) suffering	辛	辛	辛	辛	辛	辛
	辛						
立	亠	辛					

苦	kǔ (457) bitterness; pain	苦	苦	苦	苦	苦	
	苦	苦					
艹	芏	芐	苦				

瘦	shòu (†) thin	瘦	瘦	瘦	瘦	瘦	瘦
	瘦						
疒	疕	痩	瘦				

斤	jīn (847) *jin* (Chn unit of weight)	斤	斤	斤	斤		
	斤						
一	厂	斤	斤				

累	lèi (†) to be tired	累	累	累	累	累	累	累
	累							
田	罗	累						

爺	yé (387) grandfather	爺	爺	爺	爺	爺	爺	爺
	爺	爷						
父	爷	爺						

奶	nǎi (712) breasts	奶	奶	奶	奶	奶	奶	奶
	奶							
女	奶	奶	奶					

孫	sūn (†) grandson	孫	孫	孫	孫	孫	
	孫	孙					
子	孑	孫					

| | kǒu (182) mouth | | | | | | | |

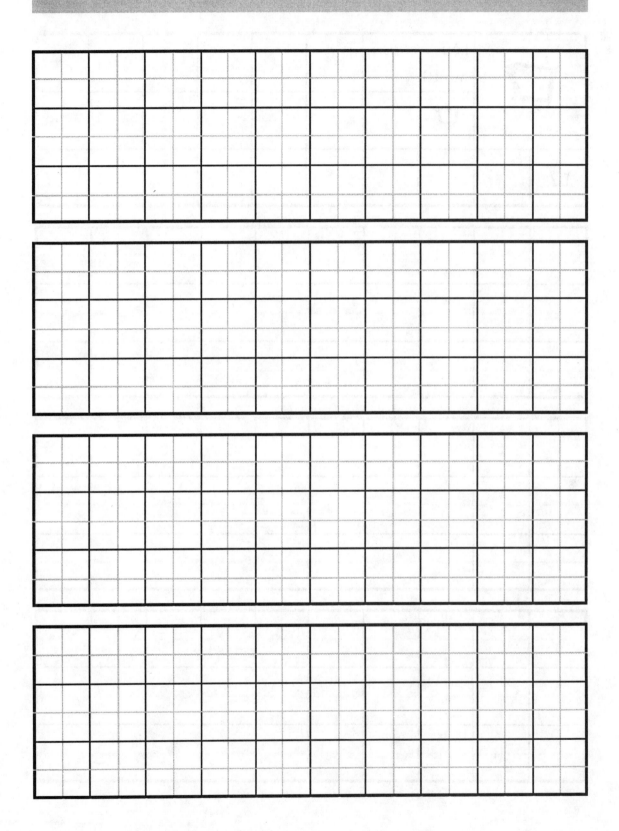

Enlarged Characters for Easier Viewing

Lesson 13	Lesson 13	Lesson 13
職	驗	續
see page 11	*see page 13*	*see page 17*
zhí	yàn	xù

Lesson 14	Lesson 15	Lesson 15
離	聰	屬
see page 20	*see page 31*	*see page 32*
lí	cōng	shǔ

Lesson 15	Lesson 16	Lesson 16
應	壞	體
see page 34	*see page 39*	*see page 41*
yīng	huài	tǐ

Lesson 16	Lesson 17	Lesson 18
癢	慶	廚
see page 42	*see page 47*	*see page 54*
yǎng	qìng	chú

Lesson 20	Lesson 20	Lesson 20
籃	壓	贏
see page 66	*see page 71*	*see page 73*
lán	yā	yíng

Lesson 21	Lesson 22	Lesson 22
韓	舊	導
see page 80	*see page 89*	*see page 92*
hán	jiù	dǎo

*	=	bound form
M	=	Measure word
P	=	Particle
QP	=	Question Particle

Lesson 12

務／务	wù	*service
桌	zhuō	table
菜／菜	cài	vegetable; dish
餃／饺	jiǎo	dumpling
素	sù	white; plain
盤／盘	pán	plate; dish
豆	dòu	bean
腐	fǔ	rotten; stale
肉	ròu	meat
碗	wǎn	bowl
酸	suān	sour
辣	là	spicy; hot
湯／汤	tāng	soup
放	fàng	put in; add
味	wèi	flavor
精	jīng	essence
渴	kě	thirsty
些	xiē	some
夠／够	gòu	enough
餓／饿	è	be hungry
傅	fù	teacher
糖	táng	sugar
醋	cù	vinegar
魚／鱼	yú	fish
甜	tián	sweet
極／极	jí	extreme
燒／烧	shāo	burn; cook

牛	niú	cow; ox
賣／卖	mài	sell
完	wán	finish
拌	bàn	mix
瓜	guā	melon
米	mǐ	rice

Lesson 13

借	jiè	borrow
帶／带	dài	belt; tape
職／职	zhí	duty; job
把	bǎ	Preposition
證／证	zhèng	evidence; certificate
留	liú	leave (behind); stay
言	yán	word
實／实	shí	reality; fact
驗／验	yàn	examine; check
樓／楼	lóu	floor; storey
忘	wàng	forget
其	qí	he; she; it; they
卡	kǎ	block; check
關／关	guān	close
門／门	mén	door; gate
剩	shèng	remain; be left over
頭／头	tóu	head
及	jí	reach
本	běn	M (for books); origin
如	rú	like; as if

果		guǒ	fruit; result
罰	罚	fá	fine; punish
續	续	xù	continue; extend
必		bì	must
須	须	xū	must
典		diǎn	standard work

Lesson 14

運	运	yùn	carry; transport
動	动	dòng	move; stir
旁		páng	side
遠	远	yuǎn	far; distant
住		zhù	live
離	离	lí	from; away
活		huó	live
心		xīn	heart
店		diàn	store shop
田		tián	(a surname); field
金		jīn	(a surname); gold
城		chéng	city; town
閉	闭	bì	close
著	着	zhe	P
眼		yǎn	eye
睛		jīng	eyeball
從	从	cóng	from
直(直)		zhí	straight
往		wàng	towards
南		nán	south
拐	拐	guǎi	turn
哎	哎	āi	Excl.
燈	灯	dēng	light; lamp
右		yòu	right
單	单	dān	one; single; odd
左		zuǒ	left

面		miàn	face; side
京		jīng	capital

Lesson 15

表		biǎo	outside; form
班		bān	class
汁		zhī	juice
接		jiē	meet; receive
林		lín	(a surname); forest
禮	礼	lǐ	gift
物		wù	thing; matter
聰	聪	cōng	acute hearing
暑		shǔ	heat; hot weather
長	长	zhǎng	grow; come into being
愛	爱	ài	love
屬	属	shǔ	belong to
狗		gǒu	dog
鼻		bí	nose
嘴		zuǐ	mouth
將	将	jiāng	going to
定		dìng	decide; fix; set
臉	脸	liǎn	face
腿		tuǐ	leg
長	长	cháng	long
指		zhǐ	finger
應	应	yīng	should; ought to
該	该	gāi	should; ought to
彈	弹	tán	play
鋼	钢	gāng	steel
琴		qín	piano
倫	伦	lún	relationship
姆		mǔ	*nurse; *maid

Lesson 16

病		bìng	illness
肚		dù	stomach; belly
疼		téng	be painful
死		sǐ	die
廁／厠		cè	lavatory; toilet
躺		tǎng	lie down
檢／检		jiǎn	inspect; examine
查		chá	inspect; examine
壞／坏		huài	bad
針／针		zhēn	needle
種／种		zhǒng	kind; type
藥／药		yào	medicine
淚／泪		lèi	tear
流		liú	flow; shed
身		shēn	body
體／体		tǐ	body
癢／痒		yǎng	itch
敏		mǐn	quick; nimble
趕／赶		gǎn	hurry; rush
越		yuè	exceed; overstep
重		zhòng	serious; heavy
健		jiàn	healthy; strong
康		kāng	well-being; health
保		bǎo	protect
險／险		xiǎn	danger; risk
猜		cāi	guess
馬／马		mǎ	(a surname); horse

Lesson 17

參／参		cān	participate
加		jiā	add; put in
印		yìn	seal; stamp

象		xiàng	appearance
演		yǎn	show; perform
費／费		fèi	spend; take (effort)
力		lì	power; strength
倆／俩		liǎ	M; two (people)
碼／码		mǎ	number
劇／剧		jù	play; opera
慶／庆		qìng	celebrate
掃／扫		sǎo	sweep
房		fáng	house; room
整		zhěng	neat; tidy
理		lǐ	tidy up; put in order
旅		lǚ	travel
係／系		xì	connection; tie
紐／纽		niǔ	button

Lesson 18

吵		chǎo	noisy
連／连		lián	even
準／准		zhǔn	acurate
備／备		bei	prepare
搬		bān	move
紙／纸		zhǐ	paper
廣／广		guǎng	broad; vast
附		fù	get close to
寓		yù	reside; live
里		lǐ	*li* (unit of length)
套		tào	suite/set
臥／卧		wò	lie (down)
廚／厨		chú	kitchen
傢／家		jiā	*furniture
俱／具		jù	all; complete
沙		shā	sand
椅		yǐ	chair

架	jià	frame; shelf
安	ān	peaceful; quiet
靜／静	jìng	quiet
非	fēi	not; no
元	yuán	*yuan* (currency)
押	yā	give as security
當／当	dāng	serve as; allow
許／许	xǔ	allow; be allowed
養／养	yǎng	raise

Lesson 19

郵／邮	yóu	mail; post
局	jú	office; bureau
寄	jì	mail; send by mail
營／营	yíng	operate; run
貼／贴	tiē	paste on; stick on
掛／挂	guà	hang
另	lìng	other
首	shǒu	head
飾／饰	shì	decorations
鮮／鲜	xiān	fresh
束	shù	M (for flowers, etc.)
訂／订	dìng	order; subscribe to
收	shōu	receive
存	cún	store; keep
支	zhī	pay out
它	tā	it
民	mín	people
幣／币	bì	currency
銀／银	yín	silver

Lesson 20

胖	pàng	fat
簡／简	jiǎn	simple

跑	pǎo	run
受	shòu	bear; receive
網／网	wǎng	net
拍	pāi	racket; slap
籃／篮	lán	basket
游	yóu	swim; travel
泳	yǒng	swim
危	wēi	danger; peril
淹	yān	flood; submerge
願／愿	yuàn	be willing
調／调	tiáo	change to; adjust
足	zú	foot
賽／赛	sài	game; match
圓／圆	yuán	round
際／际	jì	border; edge
式	shì	style; type
腳／脚	jiǎo	foot
踢	tī	kick
手	shǒu	hand
抱	bào	hold; hug
壓／压	yā	crush; press (down)
被	bèi	Preposition
擔／担	dān	carry (on a shoulder)
棒	bàng	strong; good
特	tè	special; particular
傷／伤	shāng	injure; hurt
輸／输	shū	lose (a game, etc.)
贏／赢	yíng	win (a game, etc.)

Lesson 21

計／计	jì	count; compute
劃／划	huà	plan; delimit
各	gè	each; every
護／护	hù	protect

簽／签	qiān	sign
航	háng	boat; ship; navigate
司	sī	manage; attend to
減／减	jiǎn	reduce; decrease
價／价	jià	price; value
社	shè	community; society
程	chéng	rule; order; journey
折	zhé	break; discount
頓／顿	dùn	M (for occurances)
華／华	huá	magnificent; China
初	chū	first; beginning
千	qiān	thousand
轉／转	zhuǎn	turn
內	nèi	inside
漲／涨	zhǎng	rise
盛	shèng	flourishing; abundant
韓	hán	(a surname); Korea
芝／芝	zhī	*sesame (seed)
洛	luò	(name of a river)
杉	shān	China fir
磯／矶	jī	a rock over water
香	xiāng	fragrant
港	gǎng	port; harbor

鄉／乡	xiāng	countryside
啦	lā	P
鎮／镇	zhèn	town
座	zuò	M (for bridges, etc.)
山	shān	mountain
河	hé	river
樹／树	shù	tree
滿／满	mǎn	full
風／风	fēng	wind
景	jǐng	scenery; scene
季	jì	season
滑	huá	slide
雪	xuě	snow
迎	yíng	welcome
州	zhōu	state
舊／旧	jiù	old
較／较	jiào	compare
政	zhèng	politics
濟／济	jì	help; benefit
部	bù	part; section
颳／刮	guā	blow
導／导	dǎo	lead; guide
遊／游	yóu	travel; tour

Lesson 22

父	fù	father
母	mǔ	mother
婆	pó	old woman
阿	ā	Prefix
姨	yí	aunt
親／亲	qīn	related by blood
戚	qī	relative
伯	bó	uncle
市	shì	city; market

Lesson 23

探	tàn	visit
拾	shí	pick up
提	tí	carry; raise
醒	xǐng	wake up
差	chà	wanting; short of
停	tíng	park; stop
托	tuō	ask; entrust
皮	pí	skin; leather
箱	xiāng	box; case; trunk

Integrated Chinese I, Parts 1 & 2 — Character Index
Alphabetical by Pīnyīn

*	=	bound form
M	=	Measure word
P	=	Particle
QP	=	Question Particle

A

阿	ā	Prefix	22.1
啊	a	P	6.2
哎／哎	āi	Excl.	14.2
愛／爱	ài	love	15.2
安	ān	peaceful; quiet	18

B

八	bā	eight	Num
把	bǎ	Preposition	13.1
爸	bà	dad	2.1
吧	ba	P	5.1
白	bái	white	3.1
百	bǎi	hundred	9.1
班	bān	class	15.1
搬	bān	move	18
半	bàn	half	3.1
辦／办	bàn	manage	6.1
拌	bàn	mix	12.2
幫／帮	bāng	help	6.2
棒	bàng	strong; good	20.2
保	bǎo	protect	16.2
報／报	bào	newspaper	8.1
抱	bào	hold; hug	20.2
杯	bēi	cup; glass	5.1
北	běi	north	10.2
備／备	bèi	prepare	18
被	bèi	Preposition	20.2

本	běn	M (for books)	13.2
鼻	bí	nose	15.2
筆／笔	bǐ	pen	7.1
比	bǐ	compare	10.1
必	bì	must	13.2
閉／闭	bì	close	14.2
幣／币	bì	currency	19.2
邊／边	biān	side	8.1
便	biàn	convenient	6.1
表	biǎo	outside; form	15.1
別／别	bié	other	4.2
病	bìng	illness	16.1
伯	bó	uncle	22.1
不	bù	not; no	1.3
步	bù	step	8.2
部	bù	part; section	22.2

C

猜	cāi	guess	16.2
才	cái	not until; only	5.2
菜／菜	cài	vegetable; dish	12.1
餐	cān	meal	8.1
參／参	cān	participate	17.1
廁／厕	cè	lavatory; toilet	16.1
茶／茶	chá	tea	5.1
查	chá	inspect; examine	16.1
差	chà	wanting; short of	23.1
常	cháng	often	4.1

長／长	cháng	long	15.2	當／当	dāng	serve as; allow	18
場／场	chǎng	field	11.1	導／导	dǎo	lead; guide	22.2
唱	chàng	sing	4.1	到	dào	arrive	6.1
超	chāo	exceed; surpass	23.1	道	dào	road; way	6.2
吵	chǎo	noisy	18	得	dé	obtain; get	4.2
車／车	chē	car	11.1	的	de	P	2.1
襯／衬	chèn	lining	9.1	得	děi	must; have to	6.1 (4.2)
稱／称	chēng	weigh	23.1	燈／灯	dēng	light; lamp	14.2
城	chéng	city; town	14.2	登	dēng	board	23.1
程	chéng	rule; order; journey	21.1	等	děng	wait	6.1
吃	chī	eat	3.1	弟	dì	younger brother	2.1
出	chū	go out	10.2	第	dì	(ordinal prefix)	7.1
初	chū	first; beginning	21.2	地	dì	earth	11.1
除	chú	except	8.2	點／点	diǎn	dot; o'clock	3.1
廚／厨	chú	kitchen	18	典	diǎn	standard work	13.2
楚	chǔ	clear; neat	8.2	電／电	diàn	electric	4.1
穿	chuān	wear	9.1	店	diàn	store shop	14.1
床(牀)	chuáng	bed	8.1	定	dìng	decide; fix; set	15.2
春	chūn	spring	10.2	訂／订	dìng	order; subscribe to	19.2
詞／词	cí	word	7.1	東／东	dōng	east	9.1
次	cì	M (for occurances)	10.2	冬	dōng	winter	10.2
聰／聪	cōng	acute hearing	15.2	懂／懂	dǒng	understand	7.1
從／从	cóng	from	14.2	動／动	dòng	move; stir	14.1
醋	cù	vinegar	12.2	都	dōu	all; both	2.2
存	cún	store; keep	19.2	豆	dòu	bean	12.1
錯／错	cuò	wrong; error	4.2	肚	dù	stomach; belly	16.1
				對／对	duì	correct; toward	4.1
		D		頓／顿	dùn	M (for occurances)	21.1
				多	duō	many	3.1
打	dǎ	hit; strike	4.1				
大	dà	big	3.1			**E**	
帶／带	dài	belt; tape	13.1				
單／单	dān	one; single; odd	14.2	餓／饿	è	be hungry	12.1
擔／担	dān	carry	20.2	兒／儿	ér	son; child	2.1
但	dàn	but	6.2	而	ér	and	10.1

航	háng	boat; ship	21.1
好	hǎo	fine; good; OK	1.1
號／号	hào	number	3.1
喝	hē	drink	5.1
和	hé	and	2.2
合	hé	suit; agree	9.2
河	hé	river	22.1
黑	hēi	black	9.2
很	hěn	very	3.2
紅／红	hóng	red	9.1
後／后	hòu	after	6.1
護／护	hù	protect	21.1
花／花	huā	spend	11.2
華／华	huá	magnificent; China	21.1
滑	huá	slide	22.1
話／话	huà	speech	6.1
劃／划	huà	plan; delimit	21.1
壞／坏	huài	bad	16.1
歡／欢	huān	joyful	3.1
換／换	huàn	change	9.2
黃(黄)	huáng	yellow	9.1
回	huí	return	5.2
會／会	huì	meet	6.1
活	huó	live	14.1
貨／货	huò	merchandise	9.1
或	huò	or	11.1

J

機／机	jī	machine	11.1
磯／矶	jī	a rock over water	21.2
級／级	jí	grade; level	6.1
極／极	jí	extreme	12.2
及	jí	reach	13.1
急	jí	urgent; pressing	23.1

幾／几	jǐ	QP; how many	2.2
己	jǐ	oneself	11.2
記／记	jì	record	8.1
寄	jì	mail; send by mail	19.1
際／际	jì	border; edge	20.2
計／计	jì	count; compute	21.1
季	jì	season	22.1
濟／济	jì	help; benefit	22.2
家	jiā	family; home	2.2
加	jiā	add; put in	17.1
傢／家	jiā	*furniture	18
假	jià	vacation	11.1
架	jià	frame; shelf	18
價／价	jià	price; value	21.1
間／间	jiān	M (for rooms)	6.1
檢／检	jiǎn	inspect; examine	16.1
簡／简	jiǎn	simple	20.1
減／减	jiǎn	reduce; decrease	21.1
見／见	jiàn	see	3.1
件	jiàn	M (for items)	9.1
健	jiàn	healthy; strong	16.2
將／将	jiāng	going to	15.2
教(教)	jiāo	teach	7.1
餃／饺	jiǎo	dumpling	12.1
腳／脚	jiǎo	foot	20.2
叫	jiào	call	1.2
覺／觉	jiào	feel; reckon	4.2
較／较	jiào	compare	22.2
接	jiē	meet; receive	15.1
節／节	jié	M (for classes)	6.1
姐	jiě	older sister	1.1
介	jiè	between	5.1
借	jiè	borrow	13.1
今	jīn	today; now	3.1

林	lín	(a surname); forest	15.1
另	lìng	other	19.1
留	liú	leave (behind)	13.1
流	liú	flow; shed	16.2
六	liù	six	Num
樓／楼	lóu	floor; storey	13.1
錄／录	lù	record	7.2
路	lù	road; way	11.2
旅	lǚ	travel	17.2
律	lù	law; rule	2.2
倫／伦	lún	relationship	15.2
洛	luò	(name of a river)	21.2

M

媽／妈	mā	mom	2.1
麻	má	hemp; numb	11.1
馬／马	mǎ	horse	16.2
碼／码	mǎ	number	17.2
嗎／吗	ma	QP	1.3
買／买	mǎi	buy	9.1
賣／卖	mài	sell	12.2
滿／满	mǎn	full	22.1
慢	màn	slow	7.1
忙	máng	busy	3.2
毛	máo	hair; dime	9.1
麼／么	me	*QP	1.2
沒(没)	méi	(have) not	2.1
美	měi	beautiful	1.3
每	měi	every; each	11.2
妹	mèi	younger sister	2.1
悶／闷	mēn	stuffy	10.2
門／门	mén	door; gate	13.1
們／们	men	*(plural suffix)	3.1
米	mǐ	rice	12.2

面	miàn	face; side	14.2
民	mín	people	19.2
敏	mǐn	quick; nimble	16.2
名	míng	name	1.2
明	míng	bright	3.2
末	mò	end	4.1
姆	mǔ	*nurse; *maid	15.2
母	mǔ	mother	22.1

N

拿	ná	take	23.1
哪	nǎ / něi	which	5.1
那	nà / nèi	that	2.1
奶	nǎi	breasts	23.2
男	nán	male	2.1
難／难	nán	difficult; hard	7.1
南	nán	south	14.2
腦／脑	nǎo	brain	8.1
呢	ne	QP	1.2
内	nèi	inside	21.2
能	néng	be able	8.2
你	nǐ	you	1.1
年	nián	year	3.1
唸／念	niàn	read	7.2
您	nín	you (polite)	1.2
牛	niú	cow; ox	12.2
紐／纽	niǔ	button	17.2
暖	nuǎn	warm	10.1
女	nǚ	woman; female	2.1

P

拍	pāi	racket; slap	20.1
盤／盘	pán	plate; dish	12.1
旁	páng	side	14.1

胖	pàng	fat	20.1
跑	pǎo	run	20.1
朋	péng	friend	1.2
啤	pí	*beer	5.1
皮	pí	skin; leather	23.1
篇	piān	M (for articles)	8.1
便	pián	*inexpensive	9.1
片	piàn	slice; *film	2.1
漂	piào	*pretty	5.1
票	piào	ticket	11.1
瓶	píng	bottle	5.2
平	píng	level; even	7.2
婆	pó	old woman	22.1

Q

七	qī	seven	Num
期	qī	period (of time)	3.1
戚	qī	relative	22.1
其	qí	he; she; it; they	13.1
起	qǐ	rise	5.1
氣／气	qì	air	6.1
汽	qì	steam	11.1
簽／签	qiān	sign	21.1
千	qiān	thousand	21.2
前	qián	front; before	8.1
錢／钱	qián	money	9.1
且	qiě	for the time being	10.1
親／亲	qīn	related by blood	22.1
琴	qín	piano	15.2
清	qīng	clear; clean	8.2
請／请	qǐng	please; invite	1.2
慶／庆	qìng	celebrate	17.2
秋	qiū	autumn; fall	10.2
球	qiú	ball	4.1

去	qù	go	4.1

R

然	rán	like that; so	9.2
讓／让	ràng	let; allow	11.2
熱／热	rè	hot	10.2
人	rén	man; person	1.3
認／认	rèn	to recognize	3.2
日	rì	sun; day	3.1
容	róng	hold; contain	7.1
肉	ròu	meat	12.1
如	rú	like; as if	13.2

S

賽／赛	sài	game; match	20.2
三	sān	three	Num
掃／扫	sǎo	sweep	17.2
色	sè	color	9.1
沙	shā	sand	18
衫	shān	shirt	9.1
杉	shān	China fir	21.2
山	shān	mountain	22.1
傷／伤	shāng	injure; hurt	20.2
上	shàng	above; on top	3.1
燒／烧	shāo	burn; cook	12.2
少	shǎo	few	9.1
紹／绍	shào	carry on	5.1
舍	shè	house	8.1
社	shè	community; society	21.1
誰／谁	shéi	who	2.1
身	shēn	body	16.2
什(甚)	shén	*what	1.2
生	shēng	be born	1.1
剩	shèng	remain	13.1

盛		shèng	flourishing	21.2
師／师		shī	teacher	1.3
十		shí	ten	Num
識／识		shí	to recognize	3.2
時／时		shí	time	4.1
實／实		shí	reality; fact	13.1
拾		shí	pick up	23.1
始		shǐ	begin	7.2
是		shì	be	1.3
事		shì	matter; affair	3.2
視／视		shì	view	4.1
室		shì	room	6.1
試／试		shì	try	6.1
適／适		shì	suit; fit	9.2
飾／饰		shì	decorations	19.2
式		shì	style; type	20.2
市		shì	city; market	22.1
收		shōu	receive	19.2
首		shǒu	head	19.2
手		shǒu	hand	20.2
售		shòu	sell	9.1
受		shòu	bear; receive	20.1
瘦		shòu	thin	23.2
書／书		shū	book	4.1
舒		shū	stretch	10.2
輸／输		shū	lose (a game, etc.)	20.2
屬／属		shǔ	belong to	15.2
暑		shǔ	heat; hot weather	15.2
束		shù	M (for flowers, etc.)	19.2
樹／树		shù	tree	22.1
帥		shuài	handsome	7.2
雙／双		shuāng	pair	9.2
水		shuǐ	water	5.1
睡		shuì	sleep	4.2

順／顺		shùn	in the same direction	23.1
說／说		shuō	speak	6.2
思		sī	think	4.2
司		sī	manage; attend to	21.1
死		sǐ	die	16.1
四		sì	four	Num
送		sòng	deliver	11.1
宿		sù	stay	8.1
訴／诉		sù	tell; relate	8.1
速		sù	speed	11.2
素		sù	white; plain	12.1
酸		suān	sour	12.1
算		suàn	stay	4.2
雖／虽		suī	though; while	9.2
隨／随		suí	follow	23.1
歲／岁		suì	age	3.1
孫／孙		sūn	grandson	23.2
所(所)		suǒ	*so; place	4.1

T

他		tā	he	2.1
她		tā	she	2.1
它		tā	it	19.2
台(臺)		tái	platform	10.2
太		tài	too; extremely	3.1
彈／弹		tán	play	15.2
探		tàn	visit	23.1
湯／汤		tāng	soup	12.1
糖		táng	sugar	12.2
躺		tǎng	lie down	16.1
套		tào	suite/set	18
特		tè	special; particular	20.2
疼		téng	be painful	16.1
踢		tī	kick	20.2

新		xīn	new	11.2	醫／医		yī	doctor; medicine	2.2
心		xīn	heart	14.1	衣		yī	clothing	9.1
辛		xīn	suffering	23.2	宜		yí	suitable	9.1
信		xìn	letter	8.2	姨		yí	aunt	22.1
星		xīng	star	3.1	以		yǐ	with	4.1
行		xíng	all right; O.K.	6.1	已		yǐ	already	8.1
醒		xǐng	wake up	23.1	椅		yǐ	chair	18
姓		xìng	surname	1.2	意		yì	meaning	4.2
須／须		xū	must	13.2	易		yì	easy	7.1
續／续		xù	continue; extend	13.2	因		yīn	because	3.2
學／学		xué	study	1.3	音		yīn	sound; music	4.1
雪		xuě	snow	22.1	銀／银		yín	silver	19.2
					印		yìn	seal; stamp	17.1
		Y			英／英		yīng	*England	2.2
					應／应		yīng	should; ought to	15.2
押		yā	pawn	18	迎		yíng	welcome	22.1
壓／压		yā	crush; press (down)	20.2	營／营		yíng	operate; run	19.1
呀		ya	P	5.1	贏／赢		yíng	win (a game, etc.)	20.2
淹		yān	flood; submerge	20.1	影		yǐng	shadow	4.1
顏／颜		yán	face; countenance	9.1	泳		yǒng	swim	20.1
言		yán	word	13.1	用		yòng	use	8.2
眼		yǎn	eye	14.2	郵／邮		yóu	mail; post	19.1
演		yǎn	show; perform	17.1	游		yóu	swim; travel	20.1
驗／验		yàn	examine; check	13.1	遊／游		yóu	travel; tour	22.2
癢／痒		yǎng	itch	16.2	友		yǒu	friend	1.2
養／养		yǎng	raise	18	有		yǒu	have; there is/are	2.1
樣／样		yàng	kind	3.1	又		yòu	again	10.2
要		yào	want	5.1	右		yòu	right	14.2
藥／药		yào	medicine	16.1	魚／鱼		yú	fish	12.2
爺／爷		yé	grandfather	23.2	寓		yù	reside; live	18
也		yě	also	1.3	語／语		yǔ	language	7.1
夜		yè	night	7.2	雨		yǔ	rain	10.1
業／业		yè	occupation	8.2	預／预		yù	prepare	7.1
葉／叶		yè	leaf	10.1	員／员		yuán	personnel	9.1
一		yī	one	Num					

園／园	yuán	garden	10.1
元	yuán	*yuan* (currency)	18
圓／圆	yuán	round	20.2
遠／远	yuǎn	far; distant	14.1
願／愿	yuàn	be willing	20.1
約／约	yuē	make an appoint.	10.1
月	yuè	moon; month	3.1
樂／乐	yuè	music	4.1
越	yuè	exceed; overstep	16.2
運／运	yùn	carry; transport	14.1

Z

再	zài	again	3.1
在	zài	at; in; on	3.2
糟	zāo	messy	10.2
早	zǎo	early	7.2
澡	zǎo	bath	8.1
怎	zěn	*how	3.1
站	zhàn	stand; station	11.1
張／张	zhāng	M; (a surname)	2.1
長／长	zhǎng	come into being	15.2
漲／涨	zhǎng	rise	21.2
找	zhǎo	look for; seek	4.2
照	zhào	shine	2.1
折	zhé	break; discount	21.1
者	zhě	(a suffix)	11.1
這／这	zhè(i)	this	2.1
著／着	zhe	P	14.2
真／眞	zhēn	true; real	7.2
針／针	zhēn	needle	16.1
鎮／镇	zhèn	town	22.1
整	zhěng	neat; tidy	17.2
正	zhèng	just; straight	8.1
證／证	zhèng	evidence	13.1

政	zhèng	politics	22.2
知	zhī	know	6.2
汁	zhī	juice	15.1
支	zhī	pay out	19.2
芝／芝	zhī	*sesame (seed)	21.2
職／职	zhí	duty; job	13.1
直（直）	zhí	straight	14.2
只	zhǐ	only	4.2
指	zhǐ	finger	15.2
紙／纸	zhǐ	paper	18
中	zhōng	center; middle	1.3
鐘／钟	zhōng	clock	3.1
種／种	zhōng	kind; type	16.1
重	zhòng	serious; heavy	16.2
週／周	zhōu	week	4.1
州	zhōu	state	22.1
助	zhù	assist	7.1
祝	zhù	wish	8.2
住	zhù	live	14.1
專／专	zhuān	special	8.2
轉／转	zhuǎn	turn	21.2
準／准	zhǔn	accurate	18
桌	zhuó	table	12.1
子	zǐ	son	2.1
字	zì	character	1.2
自	zì	self	11.2
走	zǒu	walk	11.1
租	zū	rent	11.1
足	zú	foot	20.2
嘴	zuǐ	mouth	15.2
最	zuì	most	8.2
昨	zuó	yesterday	4.1
左	zuǒ	left	14.2
做	zuò	do	2.2

坐   zuò   sit   5.1   座   zuò   M (for bridges, etc.) 22.1
作   zuò   work; do   5.1

Integrated Chinese, Parts 1 & 2 — Character Index
Arranged by Number of Strokes

```
*    =    bound form
M    =    Measure word
P    =    Particle
QP   =    Question Particle
```

1

一　yī　one　Num

2

八　bā　eight　Num
二　èr　two　Num
九　jiǔ　nine　Num
了　le　P　3.1
力　lì　power; strength　17.1
七　qī　seven　Num
人　rén　man; person　1.3
十　shí　ten　Num
又　yòu　again　10.2

3

才　cái　not until; only　5.2
大　dà　big　3.1
工　gōng　craft; work　5.1
女　nǚ　woman; female　2.1
己　jǐ　oneself　11.2
久　jiǔ　long time　4.2
口　kǒu　mouth　23.2
千　qiān　thousand　21.2
三　sān　three　Num
山　shān　mountain　22.1
上　shàng　above; on top　3.1
下　xià　below; under　5.1
小　xiǎo　little; small　1.1

也　yě　also　1.3
已　yǐ　already　8.1
子　zǐ　son　2.1

4

比　bǐ　compare　10.1
不　bù　not; no　1.3
方　fāng　square; side　6.1
分　fēn　penny; minute　9.1
父　fù　father　22.1
公　gōng　public　6.1
及　jí　reach　13.1
介　jiè　between　5.1
今　jīn　today; now　3.1
斤　jīn　*jin* (unit of weight)　17.1
六　liù　six　Num
毛　máo　hair; dime　9.1
内　nèi　inside　21.2
牛　niú　cow; ox　12.2
片　piàn　slice; *film　2.1
日　rì　sun; day　3.1
少　shǎo　few　9.1
什　shén　*what　1.2
手　shǒu　hand　20.2
水　shuǐ　water　5.1
太　tài　too; extremely　3.1
天　tiān　sky; day　3.1
王　wáng　(a surname); king　1.1

文	wén	script	2.2
五	wǔ	five	Num
午	wǔ	noon	6.1
心	xīn	heart	14.1
以	yǐ	with	4.1
友	yǒu	friend	1.2
元	yuán	*yuan* (currency)	18.2
月	yuè	moon; month	3.1
支	zhī	pay out	19.2
中	zhōng	center; middle	1.3

5

白	bái	white	3.1
半	bàn	half	3.1
北	běi	north	10.2
本	běn	M (for books)	13.2
必	bì	must	13.2
出	chū	go out	10.2
打	dǎ	hit; strike	4.1
冬	dōng	winter	10.2
付	fù	pay	9.1
功	gōng	skill	7.2
瓜	guā	melon	12.2
加	jiā	add; put in	17.1
叫	jiào	call	1.2
卡	kǎ	block; check	13.1
可	kě	but	3.1
另	lìng	other	19.1
民	mín	people	19.2
末	mò	end	4.1
母	mǔ	mother	22.1
皮	pí	skin; leather	23.1
平	píng	level; even	7.2
且	qiě	for the time being	10.1

去	qù	go	4.1
生	shēng	be born	1.1
市	shì	city; market	22.1
司	sī	manage; attend to	21.1
四	sì	four	Num
他	tā	he	2.1
它	tā	it	19.2
台 (臺)	tái	platform	10.2
田	tián	(a surname); field	14.1
外	wài	outside	4.1
印	yìn	seal; stamp	17.1
用	yòng	use	8.2
右	yòu	right	14.2
正	zhèng	just; straight	8.1
汁	zhī	juice	15.1
只	zhǐ	only	4.2
左	zuǒ	left	14.2

6

安	ān	peaceful; quiet	18.2
百	bǎi	hundred	9.1
吃	chī	eat	3.1
次	cì	M (for occurances)	10.2
存	cún	store; keep	19.2
地	dì	earth	11.1
多	duō	many	3.1
而	ér	and	10.1
各	gè	each; every	21.1
共	gòng	altogether	9.1
好	hǎo	fine; good; OK	1.1
合	hé	suit; agree	9.2
回	huí	return	5.2
件	jiàn	M (for items)	9.1
考	kǎo	test	6.1

老	lǎo	old	1.3
忙	máng	busy	3.2
米	mǐ	rice	12.2
名	míng	name	1.2
奶	nǎi	breasts	23.2
年	nián	year	3.1
肉	ròu	meat	12.1
如	rú	like; as if	13.2
色	sè	color	9.1
式	shì	style; type	20.2
收	shōu	receive	19.2
死	sǐ	die	16.1
她	tā	she	2.1
同	tóng	same	3.2
托	tuō	ask; entrust	23.1
危	wēi	danger; peril	20.1
西	xī	west	9.1
先	xiān	first	1.1
行	xíng	all right; O.K.	6.1
衣	yī	clothing	9.1
因	yīn	because	3.2
有	yǒu	have; there is/are	2.1
再	zài	again	3.1
在	zài	at; in; on	3.2
早	zǎo	early	7.2
州	zhōu	state	22.1
字	zì	character	1.2
自	zì	self	11.2

7

把	bǎ	Preposition	13.1
吧	ba	P	5.1
伯	bó	uncle	22.1
别／别	bié	other	4.2

步	bù	step	8.2
吵	chǎo	noisy	18.1
車／车	chē	car	11.1
初	chū	first; beginning	21.2
床(牀)	chuáng	bed	8.1
但	dàn	but	6.2
弟	dì	younger brother	2.1
豆	dòu	bean	12.1
肚	dù	stomach; belly	16.1
告	gào	tell; inform	8.1
更	gèng	even more	10.1
見／见	jiàn	see	3.1
局	jú	office; bureau	19.1
快	kuài	fast; quick	5.1
冷	lěng	cold	10.2
李	lǐ	(a surname); plum	1.1
里	lǐ	*li* (unit of length)	18.1
没(沒)	méi	(have) not	2.1
每	měi	every; each	11.2
那	nà / nèi	that	2.1
男	nán	male	2.1
你	nǐ	you	1.1
汽	qì	steam	11.1
沙	shā	sand	18.2
杉	shān	China fir	21.2
社	shè	community; society	21.1
身	shēn	body	16.2
束	shù	M (for flowers, etc.)	19.2
辛	xīn	suffering	23.2
完	wán	finish	12.2
忘	wàng	forget	13.1
位	wèi	M (polite)	6.1
我	wǒ	I; me	1.2
希	xī	hope	8.2

言	yán	word	13.1
找	zhǎo	look for; seek	4.2
折	zhé	break; discount	21.1
芝／芝	zhī	*sesame (seed)	21.2
助	zhù	assist	7.1
住	zhù	live	14.1
走	zǒu	walk	11.1
足	zú	foot	20.2
坐	zuò	sit	5.1
作	zuò	work; do	5.1

8

阿	ā	Prefix	22.1
爸	bà	dad	2.1
拌	bàn	mix	12.2
抱	bào	hold; hug	20.2
杯	bēi	cup; glass	5.1
表	biǎo	outside; form	15.1
長／长	cháng	long	15.2
到	dào	arrive	6.1
的	de	P	2.1
典	diǎn	standard work	13.2
店	diàn	store shop	14.1
定	dìng	decide; fix; set	15.2
東／东	dōng	east	9.1
兒／儿	ér	son; child	2.1
法	fǎ	method; way	7.1
房	fáng	house; room	17.2
放	fàng	put in; add	12.1
非	fēi	not; no	18.2
服	fú	clothing	9.1
附	fù	get close to	18.1
狗	gǒu	dog	15.2
拐	guǎi	turn	14.2

果	guǒ	fruit; result	13.2
和	hé	and	2.2
河	hé	river	22.1
花／花	huā	spend	11.2
或	huò	or	11.1
季	jì	season	22.1
金	jīn	(a surname); gold	14.1
京	jīng	capital	14.2
林	lín	(a surname); forest	15.1
門／门	mén	door; gate	13.1
姆	mǔ	*nurse; *maid	15.2
拍	pāi	racket; slap	20.1
其	qí	he; she; it; they	13.1
衫	shān	shirt	9.1
始	shǐ	begin	7.2
事	shì	matter; affair	3.2
受	shòu	bear; receive	20.1
所(所)	suǒ	*so; place	4.1
往	wàng	towards	14.2
味	wèi	flavor	12.1
臥／卧	wò	lie (down)	18.1
物	wù	thing; matter	15.2
些	xiē	some	12.1
姓	xìng	surname	1.2
押	yā	give as security	18.2
夜	yè	night	7.2
宜	yí	suitable	9.1
易	yì	easy	7.1
迎	yíng	welcome	22.1
泳	yǒng	swim	20.1
雨	yǔ	rain	10.1
長／长	zhǎng	come into being	15.2
直(直)	zhí	straight	14.2

9

哎／哎
保
便
查
城
穿
春
订／订
飞／飞
封
风／风
孩
很
红／红
后／后
活
计／计
架
看
客
苦／苦
亮／亮
律
洛
美
面
南
胖
便
前
秋
拾

āi	Excl.	14.2
bǎo	protect	16.2
biàn	convenient	6.1
chá	inspect; examine	16.1
chéng	city; town	14.2
chuān	wear	9.1
chūn	spring	10.2
dìng	order; subscribe to	19.2
fēi	fly	11.1
fēng	M (for letters)	8.2
fēng	wind	22.1
hái	child	2.1
hěn	very	3.2
hóng	red	9.1
hòu	after	6.1
huó	live	14.1
jì	count; compute	21.1
jià	frame; shelf	18.2
kàn	see; look	4.1
kè	guest	4.1
kǔ	bitterness; pain	23.2
liàng	bright	5.1
lù	law; rule	2.2
luò	(name of a river)	21.2
měi	beautiful	1.3
miàn	face; side	14.2
nán	south	14.2
pàng	fat	20.1
pián	*inexpensive	9.1
qián	front; before	8.1
qiū	autumn; fall	10.2
shí	pick up	23.1

是
室
首
帅
思
为／为
洗
係／系
香
信
星
要
姨
音
英／英
约／约
怎
政
指
重
祝
昨

shì	be	1.3
shì	room	6.1
shǒu	head	19.2
shuài	handsome	7.2
sī	think	4.2
wèi	for	3.2
xǐ	wash	8.1
xì	connection; tie	17.2
xiāng	fragrant	21.2
xìn	letter	8.2
xīng	star	3.1
yào	want	5.1
yí	aunt	22.1
yīn	sound; music	4.1
yīng	*England	2.2
yuē	make an appoint.	10.1
zěn	*how	3.1
zhèng	politics	22.2
zhǐ	finger	15.2
zhòng	serious; heavy	16.2
zhù	wish	8.2
zuó	yesterday	4.1

10

班
被
病
茶／茶
差
除
刚／刚
高
哥
個／个

bān	class	15.1
bèi	Preposition	20.2
bìng	illness	16.1
chá	tea	5.1
chà	wanting; short of	23.1
chú	except	8.2
gāng	just now	10.2
gāo	tall	2.1
gē	older brother	2.2
gè	M (general)	2.1

國／国	guó	country	1.3
海	hǎi	sea	10.1
航	háng	boat; ship	21.1
級／级	jí	grade; level	6.1
記／记	jì	record	8.1
家	jiā	family; home	2.2
借	jiè	borrow	13.1
酒	jiǔ	wine	5.1
俱／具	jù	all; complete	18.1
哭	kū	cry	23.1
倆／俩	liǎ	M; two (people)	17.1
留	liú	leave (behind)	13.1
流	liú	flow; shed	16.2
旅	lǔ	travel	17.2
倫／伦	lún	relationship	15.2
馬／马	mǎ	horse	16.2
們／们	men	*(plural suffix)	3.1
拿	ná	take	23.1
哪	nǎ / něi	which	5.1
能	néng	be able	8.2
紐／纽	niǔ	button	17.2
旁	páng	side	14.1
瓶	píng	bottle	5.2
起	qǐ	rise	5.1
氣／气	qì	air	6.1
容	róng	hold; contain	7.1
師／师	shī	teacher	1.3
時／时	shí	time	4.1
書／书	shū	book	4.1
送	sòng	deliver	11.1
素	sù	white; plain	12.1
孫／孙	sūn	grandson	23.2
套	tào	suite/set	18.1
特	tè	special; particular	20.2

疼	téng	be painful	16.1
夏	xià	summer	10.2
校	xiào	school	5.1
笑	xiào	laugh	8.2
員／员	yuán	personnel	9.1
站	zhàn	stand; station	11.1
真(眞)	zhēn	true; real	7.2
針／针	zhēn	needle	16.1
紙／纸	zhǐ	paper	18.1
桌	zhuó	table	12.1
租	zū	rent	11.1
座	zuò	M (for bridges, etc.)	22.1

11

啊	a	P	6.2
閉／闭	bì	close	14.2
部	bù	part; section	22.2
猜	cāi	guess	16.2
參／参	cān	participate	17.1
常	cháng	often	4.1
唱	chàng	sing	4.1
從／从	cóng	from	14.2
帶／带	dài	belt; tape	13.1
得	dé	obtain; get	4.2
得	děi	must; have to	6.1 (4.2)
第	dì	(ordinal prefix)	7.1
動／动	dòng	move; stir	14.1
都	dōu	all; both	2.2
啡	fēi	*coffee	5.1
夠／够	gòu	enough	12.1
掛／挂	guà	hang	19.1
貨／货	huò	merchandise	9.1
寄	jì	mail; send by mail	19.1
假	jià	vacation	11.1

健	jiàn	healthy; strong	16.2
將／将	jiāng	going to	15.2
教／教	jiāo	teach	7.1
接	jiē	meet; receive	15.1
康	kāng	well-being; health	16.2
啦	lā	P	22.1
淚／泪	lèi	tear	16.2
累	lèi	be tired	23.2
理	lǐ	tidy up	17.2
連／连	lián	even	18.1
涼／凉	liáng	cool	10.2
聊	liáo	chat	5.2
麻	má	hemp; numb	11.1
敏	mǐn	quick; nimble	16.2
唸／念	niàn	read	7.2
您	nín	you (polite)	1.2
啤	pí	*beer	5.1
票	piào	ticket	11.1
婆	pó	old woman	22.1
戚	qī	relative	22.1
清	qīng	clear; clean	8.2
球	qiú	ball	4.1
掃／扫	sǎo	sweep	17.2
紹／绍	shào	carry on	5.1
盛	shèng	flourishing	21.2
視／视	shì	view	4.1
售	shòu	sell	9.1
宿	sù	stay	8.1
速	sù	speed	11.2
探	tàn	visit	23.1
甜	tián	sweet	12.2
條／条	tiáo	M (for long objects)	9.1
停	tíng	park; stop	23.1
途	tú	road; way	23.1

望／望	wàng	hope; wish	8.2
問／问	wèn	ask	1.2
務／务	wù	*service	12.1
習／习	xí	practice	6.2
現／现	xiàn	present	3.2
許／许	xǔ	allow; be allowed	18.2
雪	xuě	snow	22.1
淹	yān	flood; submerge	20.1
眼	yǎn	eye	14.2
郵／邮	yóu	mail; post	19.1
魚／鱼	yú	fish	12.2
張／张	zhāng	M; (a surname)	2.1
這／这	zhè(i)	this	2.1
專／专	zhuān	special	8.2
做	zuò	do	2.2

12

棒	bàng	strong; good	20.2
報／报	bào	newspaper	8.1
備／备	bèi	prepare	18.1
筆／笔	bǐ	pen	7.1
菜／菜	cài	vegetable; dish	12.1
廁／厕	cè	lavatory; toilet	16.1
場／场	chǎng	field	11.1
超	chāo	exceed; surpass	23.1
程	chéng	rule; order; journey	21.1
詞／词	cí	word	7.1
單／单	dān	one; single; odd	14.2
登	dēng	board	23.1
等	děng	wait	6.1
發／发	fā	emit; issue	8.1
飯／饭	fàn	meal	3.1
費／费	fèi	spend; take (effort)	17.1
復／复	fù	duplicate	7.1

傅	fù	teacher	12.2	
港	gǎng	port; harbor	21.2	
給／给	gěi	give	5.1	
貴／贵	guì	honorable	1.2	
喝	hē	drink	5.1	
黑	hēi	black	9.2	
華／华	huá	magnificent; China	21.1	
換／换	huàn	change	9.2	
黃(黄)	huáng	yellow	9.1	
極／极	jí	extreme	12.2	
幾／几	jǐ	QP; how many	2.2	
傢／家	jiā	*furniture	18.1	
間／间	jiān	M (for rooms)	6.1	
減／减	jiǎn	reduce; decrease	21.1	
進／进	jìn	enter	5.1	
景	jǐng	scenery; scene	22.1	
就	jiù	just	6.1	
開／开	kāi	open	6.1	
渴	kě	thirsty	12.1	
裡／里	lǐ	inside	7.1	
買／买	mǎi	buy	9.1	
悶／闷	mēn	stuffy	10.2	
跑	pǎo	run	20.1	
期	qī	period (of time)	3.1	
琴	qín	piano	15.2	
然	rán	like that; so	9.2	
試／试	shì	try	6.1	
剩	shèng	remain	13.1	
舒	shū	stretch	10.2	
暑	shǔ	heat; hot weather	15.2	
順／顺	shùn	the same direction	23.1	
訴／诉	sù	tell; relate	8.1	
湯／汤	tāng	soup	12.1	
提	tí	carry; raise	23.1	

貼／贴	tiē	paste on; stick on	19.1	
晚	wǎn	evening; late	3.1	
喂	wèi	Hello!; Hey!	6.1	
喜	xǐ	like; happy	3.1	
鄉／乡	xiāng	countryside	22.1	
象	xiàng	appearance	17.1	
須／须	xū	must	13.2	
葉／叶	yè	leaf	10.1	
椅	yǐ	chair	18.2	
游	yóu	swim; travel	20.1	
寓	yù	reside; live	18.1	
園／园	yuán	garden	10.1	
越	yuè	exceed; overstep	16.2	
著／着	zhe	P	14.2	
週／周	zhōu	week	4.1	
最	zuì	most	8.2	

13

愛／爱	ài	love	15.2	
搬	bān	move	18.1	
楚	chǔ	clear; neat	8.2	
當／当	dāng	serve as; allow	18.2	
道	dào	road; way	6.2	
電／电	diàn	electric	4.1	
頓／顿	dùn	M (for occurances)	21.1	
煩／烦	fán	bother	11.1	
該／该	gāi	should; ought to	15.2	
跟	gēn	with	6.2	
過／过	guò	pass	11.2	
號／号	hào	number	3.1	
滑	huá	slide	22.1	
話／话	huà	speech	6.1	
會／会	huì	meet	6.1	
腳／脚	jiǎo	foot	20.2	

較／较	jiào	compare	22.2	腐	fǔ	rotten; stale	12.1
節／节	jié	M (for classes)	6.1	趕／赶	gǎn	hurry; rush	16.2
經／经	jīng	pass through	8.1	歌	gē	song	4.1
睛	jīng	eyeball	14.2	慣／惯	guàn	be used to	8.2
塊／块	kuài	piece; dollar	9.1	漢／汉	hàn	Chinese	7.1
路	lù	road; way	11.2	劃／划	huà	plan; delimit	21.1
媽／妈	mā	mom	2.1	際／际	jì	border; edge	20.2
嗎／吗	ma	QP	1.3	餃／饺	jiǎo	dumpling	12.1
腦／脑	nǎo	brain	8.1	精	jīng	essence	12.1
暖	nuǎn	warm	10.1	辣	là	spicy; hot	12.1
認／认	rèn	to recognize	3.2	練／练	liàn	drill	6.2
傷／伤	shāng	injure; hurt	20.2	綠／绿	lù	green	11.1
飾／饰	shì	decorations	19.2	滿／满	mǎn	full	22.1
睡	shuì	sleep	4.2	慢	màn	slow	7.1
歲／岁	suì	age	3.1	麼／么	me	*QP	1.2
跳	tiào	jump	4.1	漂	piào	*pretty	5.1
碗	wǎn	bowl	12.1	實／实	shí	reality; fact	13.1
想	xiǎng	think	4.2	瘦	shòu	thin	23.2
新	xīn	new	11.2	說／说	shuō	speak	6.2
爺／爷	yé	grandfather	23.2	酸	suān	sour	12.1
業／业	yè	occupation	8.2	算	suàn	stay	4.2
意	yì	meaning	4.2	圖／图	tú	drawing	5.2
遊／游	yóu	travel; tour	22.2	腿	tuǐ	leg	15.2
預／预	yù	prepare	7.1	網／网	wǎng	net	20.1
圓／圆	yuán	round	20.2	舞	wǔ	dance	4.1
運／运	yùn	carry; transport	14.1	像	xiàng	image	10.1
照	zhào	shine	2.1	學／学	xué	study	1.3
準／准	zhǔn	accurate	18.2	演	yǎn	show; perform	17.1
				銀／银	yín	silver	19.2
		14		語／语	yǔ	language	7.1
				遠／远	yuǎn	far; distant	14.1
鼻	bí	nose	15.2	漲／涨	zhǎng	rise	21.2
稱／称	chēng	weigh	23.1	種／种	zhōng	kind; type	16.1
對／对	duì	correct; toward	4.1				
罰／罚	fá	fine; punish	13.2				

15

幣／币	bì	currency	19.2
廚／厨	chú	kitchen	18.1
醋	cù	vinegar	12.2
餓／饿	è	be hungry	12.1
颳／刮	guā	blow	22.2
廣／广	guǎng	broad; vast	18.1
價／价	jià	price; value	21.1
劇／剧	jù	play; opera	17.2
課／课	kè	class; lesson	6.1
褲／裤	kù	pants	9.1
樂／乐	lè	happy	5.1 (4.1)
樓／楼	lóu	floor; storey	13.1
碼／码	mǎ	number	17.2
賣／卖	mài	sell	12.2
盤／盘	pán	plate; dish	12.1
篇	piān	M (for articles)	8.1
請／请	qǐng	please; invite	1.2
慶／庆	qìng	celebrate	17.2
熱／热	rè	hot	10.2
誰／谁	shéi	who	2.1
適／适	shì	suit; fit	9.2
彈／弹	tán	play	15.2
躺	tǎng	lie down	16.1
踢	tī	kick	20.2
調／调	tiáo	change to; adjust	20.2
線／线	xiàn	line	11.1
箱	xiāng	box; case; trunk	23.1
鞋	xié	shoes	9.2
養／养	yǎng	raise	18.2
樣／样	yàng	kind	3.1
影	yǐng	shadow	4.1
樂／乐	yuè	music	4.1

16

辦／办	bàn	manage	6.1
餐	cān	meal	8.1
錯／错	cuò	wrong; error	4.2
擔／担	dān	carry	20.2
導／导	dǎo	lead; guide	22.2
燈／灯	dēng	light; lamp	14.2
點／点	diǎn	dot; o'clock	3.1
懂／懂	dǒng	understand	7.1
鋼／钢	gāng	steel	15.2
糕	gāo	cake	10.2
館／馆	guǎn	accommodations	5.2
機／机	jī	machine	11.1
緊／紧	jǐn	tight	11.2
靜／静	jìng	quiet	18.2
錄／录	lù	record	7.2
錢／钱	qián	money	9.1
親／亲	qīn	related by blood	22.1
燒／烧	shāo	burn; cook	12.2
輸／输	shū	lose (a game, etc.)	20.2
樹／树	shù	tree	22.1
隨／随	suí	follow	23.1
糖	táng	sugar	12.2
頭／头	tóu	head	13.1
險／险	xiǎn	danger; risk	16.2
寫／写	xiě	write	7.1
醒	xǐng	wake up	23.1
澡	zǎo	bath	8.1
整	zhěng	neat; tidy	17.2
嘴	zuǐ	mouth	15.2

17

幫／帮	bāng	help	6.2
聰／聪	cōng	acute hearing	15.2
韓	hán	(a surname); Korea	21.2
磯／矶	jī	a rock over water	21.2
濟／济	jì	help; benefit	22.2
檢／检	jiǎn	inspect; examine	16.1
禮／礼	lǐ	gift	15.2
臉／脸	liǎn	face	15.2
賽／赛	sài	game; match	20.2
雖／虽	suī	though; while	9.2
鮮／鲜	xiān	fresh	19.2
謝／谢	xiè	thank	3.1
壓／压	yā	crush; press (down)	20.2
應／应	yīng	should; ought to	15.2
營／营	yíng	operate; run	19.1
糟	zāo	messy	10.2

18

簡／简	jiǎn	simple	20.1
舊／旧	jiù	old	22.1
離／离	lí	from; away	14.1
雙／双	shuāng	pair	9.2
題／题	tí	topic; question	6.1
顏／颜	yán	face; countenance	9.1
醫／医	yī	doctor; medicine	2.2
鎮／镇	zhèn	town	22.1
職／职	zhí	duty; job	13.1
轉／转	zhuǎn	turn	21.2

19

邊／边	biān	side	8.1
關／关	guān	close	13.1

壞／坏	huài	bad	16.1
藍／蓝	lán	blue	11.1
難／难	nán	difficult; hard	7.1
簽／签	qiān	sign	21.1
識／识	shí	recognize	3.2
藥／药	yào	medicine	16.1
願／愿	yuàn	be willing	20.1
證／证	zhèng	evidence	13.1

20

籃／篮	lán	basket	20.1
癢／痒	yǎng	itch	16.2
贏／赢	yíng	win (a game, etc.)	20.2
鐘／钟	zhōng	clock	3.1

21

襯／衬	chèn	lining	9.1
覺／觉	jiào	feel; reckon	4.2
覺／觉	jué	feel; reckon	4.2
護／护	hù	protect	21.1
屬／属	shǔ	belong to	15.2
鐵／铁	tiě	iron	11.1
續／续	xù	continue; extend	13.2

22

歡／欢	huān	joyful	3.1
聽／听	tīng	listen	4.1

23

體／体	tǐ	body	16.2
驗／验	yàn	examine; check	13.1

24

讓／让	ràng	let; allow	11.2

25

廳／厅   tīng   hall   8.1
灣／湾   wān   strait; bay   10.2